AGINCOURT

AGINCOURT
1415

FIELD OF BLOOD

B. Renfrew

Greenhill
Books

Greenhill
Books

First published in 2017 by Greenhill Books,
c/o Pen & Sword Books Ltd,
47 Church Street, Barnsley, S. Yorkshire, S70 2AS
www.greenhillbooks.com

© B. Renfrew 2017

ISBN 978-1-78438-212-4

Library of Congress Cataloging-in Publication Data available

Typeset by JCS Publishing Services Ltd, www.jcs-publishing.co.uk
Printed and bound in Malta by Gutenberg Press

The Story of a Battle

Agincourt: Field of Blood is a minute-by-minute retelling of one of the greatest battles of history as seen through the eyes of the men in the English and French armies on 25 October 1415. The narrative is based on contemporary accounts. All those who appear in the following pages took part in the battle or the events leading up to it.

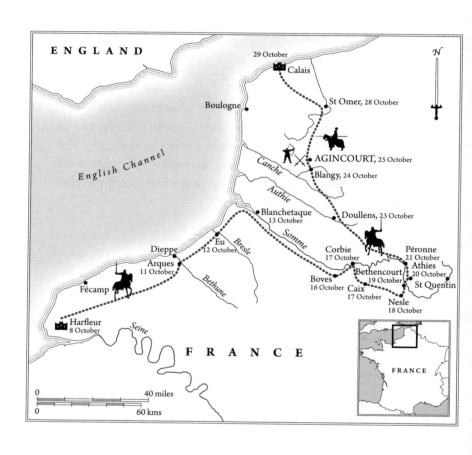

PROLOGUE

Blangy, Northern France

"They look like condemned men going to their graves," the knight grunted as he watched the passing column of English soldiers. "Not one of them thinks he will see England again."

A young monk beside him glanced up from a small prayer book; he had not found any comfort in its pages for many days. He looked at the lines of men filling the rutted track. The soldiers' faces were rigid with hunger and exhaustion, hollowed out by weeks of marching. Grey, lice-ridden skin peeked through holes in the men's ragged tunics and filthy leggings. Some of them were barefoot; blood dripped from a gash in an archer's foot, the red drops blossoming on the track like poppies in a wheat field.

A dung-brown sea of mud, broken only by clumps of lifeless trees, stretched in every direction. Dark clouds filled the iron-grey sky ahead, hurrying towards them with more of the autumn rain that had beaten down on their bowed heads and shoulders for days.

For more than two weeks the little English army had been marching across northern France, trying to reach the sea and the ships that would snatch it from destruction, but the enemy had blocked the way at every turn.

Even the lowest-born soldier had come to France with dreams of adventure, and of going home with a little honour and booty.

Now it seemed their only reward would be to leave their butchered corpses lying unburied in some French field.

"There is always hope, Sir John," Brother Thomas Elmham said. "Heaven favours our king's cause."

"Spare me your preaching, monk," Sir John Cornwall retorted. "It should have taken eight days to reach Calais. We have been marching for seventeen now. Our supplies gave out after a week, and the French have stripped the countryside bare. The men can't march much further unless we find food."

Thomas knew protest was pointless. In the abandoned villages the English soldiers found nothing but a few worm-infested apples that had fallen from the trees weeks before; only the hungriest tried to force down the rotting slime.

At that moment a tall archer stumbled from the column. The man pulled down his grimy hose as he hurried to the side of the track to relieve himself. He had gone just three steps when yellow slime exploded from his shrunken buttocks; the mess trickled down his bare thighs, coating the wool hose now bunched around his knees.

Such a spectacle would have normally brought laughter and jeers from the soldiers, but they marched past silently. Too many men had died from the sickness that had devastated the army; there was no longer any novelty in seeing a man crap himself to death.

Thomas muttered a blessing over the whimpering archer, making the sign of the cross with the prayer book. Abbot Henry had given him the volume with its beautiful hand-illustrated pages when he left the abbey at Canterbury to serve the army as a clerk. In his usual caustic way, the old man had said it would bring Thomas safely home because God would never allow so precious a thing to fall into the hands of the blasphemous French.

"Cheer up, Thomas!" boomed the knight, forgetting his own gloomy musings of a moment before. "We did not follow young Harry all this way just to lose everything."

Sir John Cornwall commanded the army's vanguard. He had been a soldier all his life, serving three English kings in the wars of Scotland, Wales and France. Stocky and of middling height, the knight's never-handsome face was leathery and battered from years of hard campaigning: his slate-grey hair was shaved almost to the scalp, and a spiky moustache framed protruding lips; one ear had been half severed by a sword stroke years before. But his light-brown eyes glinted with vigour and curiosity. Where other knights boasted of mastering wild horses and unwilling women, Sir John had a passion for learning and ideas. He had sought Thomas out after hearing of the monk's reputation as a scholar. The pair soon became one of the army's odder sights: the lanky young monk, with the perpetual smile and cornflower-blue eyes of an innocent, hurrying to keep pace with the knight's rapid stride and equally swift thoughts.

A band of Welsh archers cursed as the two men nosed their horses into the column. Sir John was amiably retorting that their mothers must have been the ugliest whores ever to work a country sheep market when shouts distracted him. A mounted scout dashed down the column, gesturing wildly behind him.

"All the world is coming against us!" cried the rider, his eyes bulging with fear.

"What is it, fellow? Talk sense!" demanded Sir John as the scout drew up.

"All of France is come," wailed the man, pointing at a nearby hill.

Curious soldiers ringed the three horsemen. Some shouted questions at the scout; others further back demanded to know what the man was saying. Sir John cursed as the clamour drowned out the scout's gibbering.

"Best we look for ourselves, Thomas," the knight called. "It will be quicker than trying to make sense of this fellow's ravings."

Forcing their horses out of the throng, the two men rode towards the hill. The army had halted even though no commands had been given; soldiers eyed the surrounding fields for signs of the enemy. Captains of the stationary contingents shouted questions as the riders passed. One young lord, flushed with his own importance, bellowed at them to halt. Sir John, flanked by men of his own retinue, galloped past without reply.

A broad plain came into view as the little band of riders reached the top of the hill. An enormous army covered the fields below: the silvery-grey armour of the advancing men resembled a mighty river snaking across the landscape. Hundreds of flags and banners flapped over the ranks of cavalry and infantry as the blare of trumpets and the beat of drums filled the air.

"Jesus save us," whispered one of the awed Englishmen. Some of the watchers mumbled prayers; others stared silently, faces frozen with disbelief and fear as they gaped at the approaching human tide.

"It seems, indeed, that all the world has come looking for us," Sir John quietly said.

Shouts and the sound of horses at their backs broke the watchers' stupor.

"Make way for the king," bellowed a knight in a surcoat emblazoned with the royal arms of England. Sir John whirled his horse around to greet the austere young man at the head of the approaching riders. His chiselled features radiated the strength of his character: firm jaw, jutting nose and narrow lips. His dark eyes took in everything, giving away nothing in return.

"What news?" called Henry of England.

Wordlessly, Sir John gestured at the plain below. Henry studied the multitude of men and horses. New detachments kept coming into view as if the French army stretched all the way to the gates of Paris, more than a hundred miles away.

"Our French cousins do us great honour by sending so many of their best men to face us," Henry said with a slight smile. From another man such words would have seemed mere foolery, but those who looked at the king saw only serenity.

"What is their number, Sir John?" the king asked.

"Not less than twenty thousand horse, sire. Every one a lord, knight or man-at-arms," came the reply. "Perhaps half that number on foot beside. I have never seen so vast a force."

"Thirty thousand, then?" Henry said. "And we but six thousand."

Sir Walter Hungerford, one of the king's knights, blurted, "I wish your majesty had another ten thousand of the finest archers in England here to aid him."

"That is a foolish way to talk," replied Henry as if gently chiding a child. "By God's mercy, I would not have one man more, even if I could."

The king paused, aware that his words would be carried back to the English army and shared with every soldier.

"I have as many men as God has seen fit to give me. My humble Englishmen will crush the arrogant French despite their enormous numbers."

A few of the lords and knights beamed at the king's words, but there was fear and doubt on the faces of most of the listeners. Thomas heard a man mutter, "Fine words for dead men."

"Summon the captains to me," cried Henry, turning his horse back to the little English force waiting on the other side of the hill. "Prepare for battle."

— PART I —

HARFLEUR

Southampton, England

None who saw it will ever forget that summer day when the English fleet set sail for France in the year of our Lord 1415. King Henry led the way in his great ship, *Trinity Royal*. The carved golden leopard at its bow lunged through the crashing waves. A white banner emblazoned with the blood-red cross of England streamed from the great mast under a radiant sun and clear blue skies. The king's ship was followed by no fewer than fifteen hundred vessels, assembled from every port and harbour in the land. The sails of the greatest ships were emblazoned with dragons, lions and other beasts that came alive, dancing and writhing, as the wind filled the cloth. It was the largest armada ever to leave English shores.

Huge warships resembling wooden castles with their fighting towers loomed over squat cargo tubs. Every vessel was crammed with men and everything an army needed to conquer a kingdom. Lords, knights and men-at-arms in helmets and breastplates of gleaming steel lined the decks; the beat of war drums and the blare of trumpets crashed over the roar of the wind and the waves; priests in robes of gold and white beseeched Heaven's blessing; the common sailors and soldiers cheered and cheered. Fortuitously, a flight of swans in the formation of an arrowhead flew low over the king's ship; men hailed it as an omen of good fortune – the

9

birds were a symbol of royalty, and their formation was said to honour the archers who made England feared on every battlefield in Europe.

It all began with such hope. Henry, the fifth of that name to rule over the English, and as great a warrior as ever had sat on the throne, dreamed of restoring his house's ancient claim to the vast domains of France. He was just twenty-eight and had barely donned the crown of England when he claimed its French twin by right of descent from his great-great-grandmother Isabella, the daughter of Philip IV of France. Wise scholars pronounced Henry's claim just, and men across the kingdom hailed the young king's boldness. They were not so lusty or cheerful when it came to finding the money to make good the claim: while most men love a good war, they are loath to pay for it out of their own purses. Parliament approved a special tax, and royal summonses went to every county to raise troops and supplies, but Henry still had to browbeat and beg his nobles, the Church and the merchants for every last penny. Even then it was not enough, and the king was forced to pawn his jewels to find sufficient coin to pay the soldiers.

An army of some fourteen thousand men from across England and Wales had assembled by early August at the port of Southampton on the southern coast. A great encampment of tents sprang up on the grassy uplands above the harbour; it was larger than any city in the kingdom except London. The army mustered two thousand men-at-arms and nine thousand archers; the remainder were grooms, servants, carters, clerks, labourers and the many craftsmen and workers an army requires. Of all the nations in Christendom, only the English depended on archers to fight their wars.

All the provisions and equipment the army would need had to be gathered from across the kingdom and brought to

Southampton by ship, in carts or on men's backs. Mountains of food, drink, weapons, tents, wagons, and arrows by the hundreds of thousands were stored on the ships. The greatest task was the loading of the army's fifteen thousand horses. Tables laid down by the royal exchequer specified how many mounts a man could take according to his rank: dukes were allowed fifty animals, earls twenty-four, barons sixteen, men-at-arms four and those archers who could afford it a single steed. Gangs of sweating and swearing sailors and grooms had to coax or force the unwilling animals to board the ships. More often than not, the beasts, kicking and screaming with fear, were winched by hand into the dark, narrow holds. Each man also had his own possessions, from the mobile chapels and iron toilets of the richest lords to the skimpy packs of the poorest archers containing a single shirt, spare leggings and a crude lead or wooden saint's emblem for protection.

Not everything had gone well in the last days before the fleet set sail for Harfleur. A plot by the earl of Cambridge to murder the king and seize the throne was uncovered; he and two other conspirators were swiftly tried and died traitors' deaths. It was a bleak reminder that more than a few questioned Henry's right to the throne because his own father had deposed King Richard. Ill-wishers and doubters whispered that the army was doomed after three ships caught fire on the eve of the fleet's departure. Even some loyal men wondered at the wisdom of the king's plans. England's peace was still precarious after the civil wars of his father's time. France might be torn by the quarrels of its own nobles, but it was still the mightiest kingdom in Europe. Was it best, the doubters muttered in the shadows, to risk England's future, and their own lives, on the daydreams of a youth? Such doubts soon seemed like wisdom.

—— **22 SEPTEMBER** ——

Harfleur, Northern France, 12:00 p.m.

Shortly after midday, the gates of the great French port of Harfleur were opened. Moments later, the flag of England was raised above the town's shattered battlements. Exhausted survivors of the French garrison abandoned the posts they had held for more than six weeks. English soldiers swiftly took possession of the town as the terrified inhabitants barricaded themselves inside their homes with tables, chairs and whatever could be piled against the wooden doors; no one trusted the hated English to keep their promise not to sack the now-defenceless town.

Once English control had been imposed, a single trumpet call sounded from the king's camp outside the walls. Harfleur's commander and its chief citizens emerged in a single file from the town's main gate. Each man wore only a long white shirt reaching to his knees; rope nooses hung from their necks as if they were criminals going to the gallows. With heads bent, the men walked barefoot between lines of jeering English soldiers. Each step the little band took was marked with a roll of drums. Slowly the captives walked through the siege lines, past the emplacements holding the great cannons that had battered the city, past the trenches where the attackers had sheltered during the siege, before climbing a muddy slope to the English camp. There the men knelt before the king as he sat on a throne in full armour. Henry admonished the prisoners for defying him as their rightful ruler, but then granted the populace of the fallen city their lives.

"It's a pantomime," grimaced Lord Camoys as he watched grinning English men-at-arms mocking the prisoners by drawing grubby fingers across their own throats in slicing motions. "Like one of those morality plays that terrify children and village idiots."

"Perhaps," murmured Sir Thomas Erpingham.

Camoys glanced at the knight. "You doubt it? It is no secret that the garrison agreed to surrender a week ago if they were not reinforced. Otherwise we would still be sitting on our arses in the mud while they taunted us from the walls. This is no triumph."

"Taking Harfleur was never going to be the easy victory our untried young gallants expected," replied Erpingham. "They had to learn that war is not like the fairy tales they listened to as children. They've been blooded, and now they need to feel they have won a victory, no matter how trifling. Which is why the king has staged this little drama, as you put it. It will help turn them into a real army."

And yet Erpingham could not deny in his own thoughts that the confidence which sped the English fleet out of Southampton had begun to crumble the moment the coast of France was sighted. The army had only learned on sailing that its destination was Harfleur on the coast of Normandy. It was one of France's most important ports, and a haven for raiders who had preyed on English ships in the adjoining channel for years, plundering their cargoes, abducting rich passengers for ransom and tossing the gutted bodies of the crews into the waves.

Many in the army had expected Harfleur to surrender at the mere sight of an English force outside its walls. Instead, the French had beaten the attackers back for six weeks even though the town's two miles of walls were held by a handful of men. It had taken a month of battering by the English guns and several bloody assaults to break the will of the garrison and the populace. Even then the French refused to surrender immediately, agreeing only to yield if a relief force had not appeared by an agreed date. Henry had agreed rather than pay the butcher's bill of yet another attack on the town's still strong defences.

"You do not look well, my lord." There was concern in Erpingham's voice as he studied his companion's narrow features.

Camoys was a sardonic and difficult man, but he was also an excellent soldier and strategist. "You are not ill, I trust."

"Have no fear, Sir Thomas, it is just a passing discomfort. My tent lies close to the marshes, and my physician tells me that the vapours which seep from their depths at night disturb the chest."

"Not the bloody flux then? I am glad."

Camoys greeted the question with his habitual barking laugh. "No. I still have control of my bowels."

A French army might not have arrived to save Harfleur, but another, invisible, force had risen to the aid of the beleaguered fortress. A great pestilence broke out in the English ranks almost as soon as the first soldier set foot on the beach. Thousands of men were struck by the bloody flux. The sick fouled themselves a dozen times or more a day, lying helpless like newborns in pools of their own waste; most died in agony. The affliction had no respect for rank, and earls and bishops suffered as much as the lowest kitchen hands. Some of the wiser English physicians said the flux was a disease of armies caused by many men living packed tightly together amid the filth from the lavatory pits and the decaying corpses of humans and animals killed in the fighting. Others said it was a sign of God's disfavour. Whatever the cause, the physicians could not cure the affliction. Soon it seemed that only the dying would be left to bury the dead.

"What of the state of the army? Have we a reckoning of our losses from the sickness?" Erpingham asked.

Camoys' watery grey eyes showed no emotion as he replied. "It seems the death count is close to two thousand, with an equal number too sick or broken to be of further use."

"That is more than a third of the army," Erpingham blurted. "Far more than I feared."

"Indeed," Camoys sombrely responded. "Many great nobles and knights will never see England again. At least the pestilence is lessening."

"And the duke of Clarence?" Erpingham asked; the king's brother had been ill for days.

"I am told by good authority that he will live, although the king has decided to send the duke to England to speed his recovery."

"That is good, although his absence will be a loss to the army. The duke is a fine soldier."

"Aye, but the rest of us may soon follow him. Winter comes on, and the campaign season is almost done. We cannot stay here for much longer."

"Has the king spoken of his intentions?"

"Good sir, you credit me with a standing far beyond my station," replied Camoys in his usual mocking tone. "Our young king shares his thoughts with no one."

—— 23 SEPTEMBER ——

Leure Gate, Harfleur, 10:00 a.m.

Henry halted his horse and dismounted before the main gate of Harfleur. One of the two stone towers flanking the entry had collapsed from the pounding of the English siege guns; the huge, grey granite stones lay in heaps like abandoned toy blocks. Ash from the fire-blackened tower wafted into the nostrils and mouths of the king and his escort. It helped mask the putrid reek of decomposing corpses.

"Sire, will you not ride?" asked a page holding the king's horse.

Henry dismissed the query with a single shake of his head. "This victory is God's work. It is not for me to ride in triumph through the town as a conqueror."

Henry walked slowly through the gate. The cobblestone street was littered with arrows and debris. Some of the fronts of the brick and timber buildings had collapsed from the bombardment, revealing the shattered chambers and rooms within to the gaze of the king and his escorts. A few old women in rags hunted for food amid the wreckage. They vanished through doorways when they saw the armoured men. There was no other sign of life.

"Come, my lords. There is no danger here." Henry sheathed his sword.

Without another word, the king led the way to the battered Church of Saint Martin in the centre of the town. Its crosses and other valuables had been sent to safety when the first English soldiers were sighted from the walls. A single candle now illuminated the long, empty nave. Henry crossed himself at the door before walking to the altar, where he knelt on the granite floor.

The king of England prayed alone before the bare wooden table, head bent over his steepled hands. Three royal chaplains standing behind him softly recited the Te Deum. The Latin words of the great prayer reverberated inside the echoing emptiness of the church as the king's entourage silently stood guard in the shadows.

Some of those who were in the church said later that it was more like a funeral mass than a thanksgiving for a victory. Nor was there much jubilation in the army. If a single town was so difficult to take, many asked, how could they hope to conquer all of France? Some talked of going home before winter. Those still full of fight said they would not return to England until they had won a full share of honour and glory, and a few bags of French coins. Besides, they added, the army would be mocked if it went back with so little to show for its efforts. And when the men had talked and bickered themselves silent, the army waited to see what the king would decide, for they knew that it was his decision alone.

Harfleur, Shortly After Noon

"Come out, you French curs!"

The command was met by silence. Humphrey, the duke of Gloucester, pointed with an armoured fist at the door of a large merchant's house. "Knock it down."

Humphrey watched idly from his horse as three soldiers with hammers smashed the thick wooden door to jagged shards before forcing their way inside. They reappeared moments later, dragging a white-bearded man and two crying women out into the street. With a shove, one of the soldiers sent the man sprawling on his hands and knees in front of the duke's horse; the bored animal barely glanced at the whimpering figure grovelling at its hooves.

"Please, my lord, have mercy. We are poor people with no gold or silver. Spare us for the love of God and his Holy Mother." The man clasped his hands together as he knelt on the cobblestones. Both of the women sobbed; one was elderly, but the other was about twenty, and more than pleasing, thought the soldier holding her.

"Silence," Humphrey barked. "All of your movable goods are forfeit to the crown. Show my men where your money box is hidden. Hide nothing if you wish to live." A clerk translated the duke's command into French.

With a curt nod to the soldiers, Humphrey trotted down the street. While the king gave thanks in the main church, his younger brother had been handed the more earthly task of stripping the town of its wealth to fill the empty royal coffers. Henry had spared the populace's lives, but he demanded their wealth as the price for defying him.

"Come out!" Humphrey bellowed as he clattered along the uneven cobbles. People who had watched from behind closed shutters as the door of their neighbour was smashed now unlocked their own entrances. Soldiers poured into the homes, pounding on walls and floors, searching for hiding places, as others roughly ran their hands over the inhabitants, tearing away purses and the richer garments. Clerks with wax tablets and wooden styluses methodically listed the loot as it was piled in the street.

* * *

That was only the start of Harfleur's suffering that day. Henry had ordered the expulsion of most of the populace. The French would try to retake the town, and it would be easier for the new English garrison to hold out if there were fewer mouths to feed and less risk of an uprising at their backs. Hundreds of women and children sobbed and shrieked, alternately pleading with and cursing the impassive English soldiers driving them through the streets. Amid them stumbled the town's cripples, the blind and the insane. Each adult was allowed to take only a small bundle of clothing and food, and no more than five sous, the smallest French coin. Some of the poorest women had shrieked scornfully that they did not possess a single sou.

"A foul business," said a knight of the royal household as he rode back to the English camp that evening after the last wretches had been driven from the town.

"The people got off lightly," said his older companion.

"Lightly? Driven out into the wilds to endure God knows what?" the younger man demanded.

"Would you rather the worst of our men had been given three days to slaughter and rape as the laws of war allow for refusing to surrender?" was the unemotional reply.

"And what of mercy? Is there no room for that in our hearts?"

"Mercy is God's business," the other knight replied. "Ours is war."

King Henry's Tent, 7:34 p.m.

That evening Henry summoned Raoul de Gaucourt, the French knight who had commanded the Harfleur garrison. Only Henry, his brother the duke of Gloucester, four other men of high rank and a single page were present when the prisoner was ushered into the king's tent. Oil lamps suspended on chains cast a subdued yellow light; an iron brazier heaped with red coals provided warmth against the sea wind. De Gaucourt gave no sign of awe or apprehension as he looked around. Tall and lithe, he regarded the Englishmen with lively hazel eyes that were accustomed to finding the world both interesting and amusing. He wore a plain light-blue tunic with the embroidered arms of his house on the left breast.

"Sir, you are welcome," Henry greeted him in oddly accented French that de Gaucourt realised must hark back to the Norman origins of the king's ancestors. "You will take wine?"

Unbidden, the page poured a rich red draft from a silver jug into a matching goblet and carried it with both hands to the Frenchman. De Gaucourt accepted it with a small bow to the king. Raising the cup to his lips, de Gaucourt studied the tent over the rim as he sipped. It was austere, with none of the comforts and trinkets that even a minor French lord took on campaign. A large wooden cross and shields hanging from the tent posts were the only decoration. An altar stood at the far end. Henry's piety was extraordinary even in an age when every man lived in fear and wonder of Heaven; it was well known that the king often attended services three times a day.

De Gaucourt took in the faces of the men arrayed around the king. All were dressed in red and gold silks and satins in stark contrast to Henry's plain black doublet and hose; he surmised they were members of the king's council.

"You are well?" the king enquired as de Gaucourt looked up from the wine.

"As well as a captive may be, sire."

Henry raised his own goblet. "The fortunes of war. I hope yours may soon recover."

"At the cost of my fortune," quipped de Gaucourt, ironically referring to the fact he was a prisoner until his freedom was secured with a ransom that would probably bankrupt his family.

There was no bitterness in de Gaucourt's voice. Ransoms were as much a part of war as broken heads, and less fatal.

"You conducted a brave defence," Henry changed the subject.

"My thanks, sire. Your own reputation as a warrior is well known."

Henry, always quick to praise the deeds of others, but never comfortable at receiving compliments, brusquely waved aside the tribute. "It is said the garrison numbered no more than a thousand men?"

"Far less," de Gaucourt answered with a shake of his head. "We were not even four hundred."

Henry frowned, although it was not clear if it was at the Frenchman's answer or the snort of derision from his brother.

"Indeed, we had less than four hundred men," de Gaucourt calmly affirmed, staring at Gloucester. "Harfleur had a standing garrison of seventy men-at-arms and crossbowmen. The city would not have lasted a day had I not arrived with three hundred lances before your army had completed its encirclement."

"And yet you fought well for so few against so many," the king remarked.

"We were aided by the townsfolk. Our people regard you English as devils who will ravish their wives, eat their children and take all that they possess. Even the most timid shopkeeper would rather fight than fall into your hands."

The French knight's words rankled several of the English lords, but the king showed no sign of irritation.

"And yet we showed mercy to them even though they had no right to expect it," he said after a pause.

"And I thank you, sire, but the enmity between our peoples is both very old and very bitter. English armies have laid waste to France many times, destroying her towns and villages, killing her people and plundering her wealth. Hatred of the English runs deep in the veins of all good Frenchmen."

"And fear," jeered Gloucester.

"True." De Gaucourt was unperturbed by the taunt. "Any man who has ever been on a battlefield knows fear, unless he is mad or a simpleton, but most of us still find sufficient courage to fight you."

"Let us not resume the battle here," Henry soothed. "This good knight is our guest, my lords. We should not complain when he gives an honest answer to our questions. Come, de Gaucourt, join us at table."

With that the king rose and strode to a table where a meal of roast meats, cheese, bread and fruit was laid out. Henry indicated de Gaucourt should sit next to him as the others took seats. The king was served first, but before taking a bite he lifted a hunk of meat from his platter on the point of a knife, handing it to the Frenchman. It was an extraordinary honour for any man to be served by a king, and de Gaucourt's descendants would talk of it for generations, even if it had come from an Englishman.

Henry said nothing until the other men at the table had satisfied their hunger. He had eaten little, merely picking at the modest portion he had taken.

"You have served at the court of our cousin Charles?"

"King Charles, the ruler of France," answered de Gaucourt.

Henry acknowledged the knight's loyalty to his French rival with another half-smile.

"I would like you to take a message to our cousin in Paris, or more precisely to his son Louis, who claims he is crown prince – or dauphin, as you call it."

"And the message, sire?"

"A challenge to single combat."

"Sire?" De Gaucourt showed uncertainty for the first time.

"I say that I am the true king of France. Charles says otherwise. Let us then put the matter in God's hands and decide it with our swords. Why should thousands of honest men die needlessly?"

"Single combat? You would fight the king?" de Gaucourt blurted.

"Our cousin is old and touched by an unfortunate malady," said Henry, referring to the French ruler's intermittent madness which made him believe he was made of glass and would shatter if touched. "No, we will fight Louis."

De Gaucourt could not conceal his astonishment. Two princes meeting in single combat to decide the fate of kingdoms was the stuff of legends. And the notion of Louis, a fat, indolent nineteen-year-old, facing this practised English killer in mortal combat was too embarrassing for the Frenchman to imagine. Louis preferred lifting the skirts of simple-minded kitchen maids to even touching a sword

"This is no small thing I ask," Henry continued after giving the French knight a moment to master his thoughts. "You are unlikely to receive a warm welcome in Paris. Some will suggest that you failed to do your duty by not leaving your bones in Harfleur."

"Those who judge fairly will know we held out for longer than could be expected. And those who criticise would be the last to risk their own necks," de Gaucourt replied. "I will take your message to Paris, sire, although I suspect we both know the answer."

"Perhaps, but God expects us to try. There is nothing more grievous in the eyes of Heaven than to see Christian people slaughter each other."

—— **24 SEPTEMBER** ——

Sir John Cornwall's Tent, 6:32 a.m.

Word of Henry's challenge to the French crown prince raced through the English camp; by morning every man and boy knew of it. Those who loved Henry beamed with pride and pleasure;

others who had been unsure of him swallowed their doubts; any who were not friends of the king gritted their teeth and pretended to join in the jubilation.

"Will the king truly fight the French prince?" Thomas asked Sir John as they broke their fast on a day-old loaf of bread that was barely enough for one man, and an even smaller jug of sour red wine. Food was becoming scarce in the camp as the onset of the autumn storms interrupted shipping from England.

"Oh, he would fight," the knight replied through a mouthful of wine-softened bread. "Not that the French foot-licker will ever show up. It is said he does not rise from his bed until well past noon, and the thought of blood makes him swoon."

"Then why does the king challenge him?"

"You're the one in the miracle business, monk. Perhaps the Almighty will decide to stiffen the frog's prick so that Harry can chop it off, and we can all go home."

The monk blushed at the knight's mockery. "I do not understand," Thomas persisted. "If the king knows the French prince will not fight, then surely the army is wrong to rejoice."

"Not at all, you puppy." Sir John noisily slurped a mouthful of wine from the jug. "This is piss," he grimaced. "Although, God knows when we will get better."

The knight tugged another strip from the loaf, and thoughtfully chewed for a moment. "Our king knows full well that fat goose of a French princeling will not fight," he finally said. "But Henry's play-acting with this challenge has cheered the army, and bought him some time."

"Time for what?" Thomas got in as the knight swallowed the last of the bread.

"To build support for whatever it is that he is planning. Henry is determined not to go back to England with so little to show. It will only stir up his enemies. There is a tide of treason straining to break free at the first chance. That whelp Cambridge was the least of the king's enemies," said Sir John, referring to the plot at Southampton.

"Then we will not go home soon?" Thomas could not hide his despondency.

"Perhaps never" cheerfully answered the knight as he brushed the crumbs from his beefy palms.

—— **5 OCTOBER** ——

The King's Tent, 3:12 p.m.

Henry studied his council. Nearly two weeks had passed since de Gaucourt had left for Paris with the challenge to the dauphin. There had been no word from him or the French. The royal council had assembled to decide what the army should do.

Children and common folk believe a king has only to flick his smallest finger to be obeyed, but even the strongest ruler is wise to seek the advice of his nobles and win their support with persuasion rather than brusque commands. England's kings had better reason to know this than most rulers: turbulent barons had deprived more than one of their supposedly supreme lords of both his throne and his life.

The king gazed at the men around the table. He could tell the mood of each one of them with a single glance. His cousin, Edmund, the duke of York, was stony faced as usual. He was the richest landowner in England, with power second only to the king's. Some of Henry's close friends distrusted York because he was cold and aloof – and had a claim by blood to the throne – but he served the king loyally.

Seated on Henry's other side was the youngest of his three brothers, Humphrey. He was sulkily fiddling with a red garnet ring the size of a pigeon's egg; it made his long, delicate fingers seem even more womanly. Poor Humphrey, Henry thought, he yearns to win glory leading armies to great victories, but he is weak and will never be a great leader.

Henry's gaze wandered down the table, taking in the earls of Dorchester, Oxford and Arundel. The last was deathly pale from the flux, only able to sit up with the aid of cushions packed into the sides of his chair; he had asked for the king's permission to return home and was to leave in the next day or so. At the end of the table were the men with lesser titles, including Sir John Cornwall.

Henry saw doubt and weariness in varying measure in all of the faces around him. Most were good men and stout soldiers, he thought, but all were uneasy. The siege of Harfleur had taken far longer than expected, and there was little to show for all the effort and expense of the expedition. And now with winter coming on, and supplies running low, many of the council feared disaster if the army remained in France.

"The fighting season is done." A plump northern baron, known more for his love of comfort than campaigning, was speaking in a nasal whine. "It is time to go home, my lords, and plant heirs on our good wives or sow bastards as the fancy may take us."

The bumbling attempt at humour earned few smiles.

Henry caught York's eye. The rest of the council, oblivious of the king's signal, straightened in their seats as the duke stood.

"Sire," York drily began, "it is true the fighting season is almost done. Winter is coming, and the army must return to England. We have neither the money nor the supplies to stay in France. The only question is when we leave and from where." York paused to give weight to what he would say next. "We can embark from Harfleur or Calais. Leaving from Harfleur will not be easy. The harbour here was damaged in the siege. Calais is secure, with ample shipping to hand."

Every head nodded in agreement. Calais was one of the greatest ports in France, and, even better, was English territory, captured in the wars of Edward III almost seventy years before. The army would be safe if it reached its walls.

"It will take eight days to reach Calais. Once there the army can be shipped safely home with as much time as is needed," York concluded.

"And what of the French?" the earl of Arundel interjected. "Will they just let us march across their country? We have lost many men, and a sizable garrison will have to be left to hold Harfleur if the enemy are not to retake it as soon as the army is out of sight."

Arundel looked at the king. "Sire, I shall be dead soon enough, so let me speak frankly."

"We are never dismayed to hear honest council," Henry replied.

"I hope that I may go to my grave knowing that I have served you faithfully," the earl replied. "Indeed, now the moment comes near, I find death holds little fear, but still I would not urge other men to rush to its embrace. To march to Calais is to risk disaster. Every day our agents bring reports of a French army gathering to the east while our forces dwindle. Would your majesty risk everything by marching through a hostile land where we can hope for neither reinforcements nor supplies?" Arundel paused before adding, "This army is the only one that England possesses. We will not raise a second if it is lost."

Several of the councillors nodded at the old man's candour.

Predictably, it was Humphrey who protested: "What is there to fear from craven French coxcombs? They have not dared lift a finger since we came to France."

Arundel answered with the serenity of a man who knew that he no longer had any stake in the world. "It is true that the French have not moved against us here, but they have lost little by it while the siege bled us more than we can afford. An English army marching across France, however, is a very different matter. Charles and his nobles could not ignore such a challenge. To go to

Calais will almost certainly mean meeting a much larger French army on a field of their choosing. God doubtless favours our king, and the rightness of his cause, but a single mistake may cost the lives of every man in the army."

Arundel's last words fell on the council like a burial shroud being unfurled on a new corpse. All of them had seen skirmishes and sieges, but great battles were rare even if the songs of minstrels made them seen as common as rosy dawns in summer. Armies risked battles only if they were sure of victory or had no choice; too much could go wrong.

Henry broke the silence. "My lords, I thank you all for your council. I have listened carefully, and there is much merit in what each of you has said. There is no shame when wise men urge prudence. And yet we are minded to go and see something of our French kingdom before returning to England. With Heaven's aid, we shall march to Calais, and if the French try to stop us, we shall not run away."

—— **6 OCTOBER** ——

English Camp, Harfleur, Mid-Afternoon

Thomas stared miserably at the roll of yellow parchment spread out on a barrel top. A burly steward, his breath stinking of raw onion and rotting teeth, stood on the other side of the makeshift table, stabbing at the empty sheet with a red finger as thick as a sausage.

"None of your weedy excuses, brother. You've had half the day to reckon how many whoresons there are in the Cheshire bands," the steward snarled.

A head count of the army had been ordered as part of preparations for the march to Calais. Thomas and the other priests, among the few men in the camp who could read, write and handle figures, had been given the task.

27

"I have asked their captain again and again," Thomas tried to explain. "And yet I do not comprehend one word in ten of what they say."

"Have you tried Latin?" the steward asked.

Thomas started to explain why that would not work before realising the man was mocking him. The stewards were practical men with little time for soft-handed priests who could not tell you how many carts of bread or barrels of beer a thousand archers needed to survive a week on the march. Besides, the clergy who kept the royal account books tended to take a dim view of the pilfering that all stewards regarded as a God-given right – either that or they demanded an outrageous share of the pickings in return for their silence.

"Go back and scare the daylights out of that sheep-shagging northern scum," the steward said. "It's that or explain to the chamberlain why not."

Thomas rolled up the parchment and glumly walked to where the Cheshire archers camped. Raising an army was a business venture like any other in which the investors shared the costs and the risks. While the king recruited some troops, most of the army was raised by nobles and captains, who agreed to provide a certain number of men-at-arms and archers for a set fee. Terms and rates of pay were set out in contracts with the throne.

The English camp was disappearing as the army prepared to march. Hundreds of servants and grooms packed gear into chests and loaded supplies onto horses and wagons. Fletchers, skilled men who made and repaired arrows, inspected bundles, each containing a hundred and forty-four of the deadly yard-long projectiles; smiths sharpened swords and knives on grinding wheels, their bent heads and shoulders engulfed in showers of yellow sparks.

As he walked through the bustle, Thomas went over his earlier exchanges with the captain of the Cheshire archers, a short, dark

man with a cheerful weather-beaten face resembling the colour
and texture of his battered brown leather jerkin.

"How many men have you, my good fellow?" the monk had
enquired.

His question was answered with a spate of unfathomable
sounds. Perplexed, the monk had tried various ploys, first talking
slowly and exaggerating his words, as if speaking to a backward or
very young child, and then almost shouting, as the English tend
to do when addressing a foreigner. Each question was answered
with more cheerful gibberish.

"Brother!"

A man beckoned Thomas over to a cart where sweating archers
stripped to the waist were loading sacks of flour.

"Captain Alderton," Thomas greeted the man. Robert Alderton
was one of the army's low-born captains; their military expertise
outweighed their lack of a title or noble birth that was the usual
requirement for a command. The captain led a company of
Buckinghamshire archers considered one of the best in the army.
Alderton was in his early thirties, of middling height with fair hair
shaved close to the scalp. Like most of the army's veterans, his eyes
never seemed to blink. He was dressed in typical archer's garb with
a leather tunic, a grey wool shirt, brown wool leggings and a brown
wool hood, which now hung on his back. The only outward signs
of rank were a stout pair of well-made leather boots, and the large
purse hanging from a broad belt with a wide brass buckle.

Thomas had seen the archer labouring over a list of stores earlier in the day: the pen was gripped in the man's clenched fist as
if it was a snake trying to bite him. Offering to help, the monk
had transformed the squiggles and blots into spotless columns
of figures.

"I did hear your words with that lard belly of a steward. Here, take
this. It will make even a heathen speak clearly," Alderton said now.

A heavy leather flask was thrust into the monk's right hand. Thomas could smell the sharp tang of the potent liquor the French called brandy wine. It brought a high price in the English army; the soldiers said the cheerful indifference it induced to any kind of misery and suffering made it one of the few things worth having in France.

Thomas frowned at the heavy flask.

"This is kind of you, Master Alderton, although I am not sure that a tipsy head will aid me in completing my task."

"Bless your balls, brother," laughed the archer, his amusement only increased by Thomas's reddening cheeks. "It's not for you, but them lumpish northerners. To loosen their tongues, like."

"Ah. I think I understand," Thomas said. He studied the flask for a moment; the liquid sloshed from side to side as he considered an idea that had been nagging him for days.

"It is good of you, Master Alderton, but I think you may help me in another way."

"How so, brother?"

"I believe I could do my duties better if I understood the men. That is, if I knew something of their nature," Thomas explained.

Alderton's smile crimped in to the wary look of a man who suspects he is being mocked.

"Understand common soldiers? You, a holy man who passes his days attending to the king's affairs?"

"I am writing an account of the campaign. I wish to understand more of the men so that I may tell something of their story," the monk eagerly explained.

"Tell the story of cutthroats, whore masters and thieves?" gasped Alderton. "Write it down, you mean? In a book? Nay, brother, such things are only done with saints and kings, not the vermin in the ranks."

It was the monk's turn to look pained. "The Bible teaches that every man has his part to play in God's kingdom, no matter how small. Of course, the deeds of the king and his great lords matter most, and yet I do not see why some mention cannot be made of the good, stout-hearted fellows who serve them."

"Well, one or two in the army may fit that description, although I've yet to meet them. Still, you are a learned man and must know what you're about. What do you wish to know?"

Thomas hesitated as dozens of questions jostled in his mind.

"What kind of men join the king's army? Commoners, that is," he said after a moment's thought.

"Well, now. You have set me a pretty piece of work. What kind of man goes to the wars?" The archer motioned to the monk to sit on a beer keg while settling on its twin. "There's no single answer to that, brother." Alderton spoke with care. "Rather there may be as many answers as there are men in the army. Each has his own reasons. It is not an easy calling, and many who answer it pay with their lives. But for all that, there's no want of fellows eager and willing to serve. Not that there's many who know what they are getting into."

Alderton hesitated again as he searched for words.

"Many go to the wars because it is their duty. A lord raises soldiers from among his tenants and retainers who must do service in return for land or their keep. An earl with vast estates will raise scores of men while a humble squire who has but a single farm will bring only two or three men."

Thomas nodded. "So they are compelled to serve?"

"Aye. It is their duty, but it's also an honour. A lord does not willingly go to war with oafish peasants who can only use a blunt blade to hack at their bread – that is the quickest way to get himself killed. No, he takes his best, men of some standing with courage and skill at arms, and they are proud to go."

"Some of the archers do not serve in a lord's following, but enlist as free men of their own will," Thomas interjected.

"True. Many of them serve for the pay, especially those from the marches or border lands close to Wales and Scotland. The soil in those parts is poor for farming so men make ends meet with raiding across the borders, which helps make them fine soldiers. And the king pays good money to serve in his army. An archer receives sixpence a day – half as much as a knight. That's as much as a peasant works half a year to see."

"And you, Master Alderton, how came you to be a soldier?"

"That is easy to answer, brother. I was raised to it. My grandfather was the first to go to the wars in the time of old King Edward. He was restless and wanted to wander a bit. He was also a fine archer, and the crown needed men for the French wars. So he served at the great Battle of Crecy with the king and his noble son, the Black Prince. That was a terrible fight, where the French first learned the power of our longbows. Thousands of them died that day. My father trod the same path because he grew up hearing his own father's tales. And then I followed him. So you might say it's a family trade. And there are more than a few families like ours."

"Do the wars make men wealthy?" Thomas's question brought a gust of laughter.

"Soldiering is more likely to leave a man penniless. Each soldier must provide his weapons and often a horse. Then he must pay for food and lodgings. And the crown can be very slow to pay wages and the like. I know men who are still waiting for their pay from the campaigns of the king's late father. But if you survive the wars, and live long enough, you're likely to get a few shillings for your old age. And there are other ways by which hardy men may hope to fatten their purses."

"How so?"

"There's always a bit of loot, and most soldiers dream of capturing a rich lord to ransom. There was a Norfolk squire who captured a French duke in the wars of King Edward. They do tell as how he won a ransom of ten thousand pounds, or as much as the king himself draws in a year or two from the whole of the kingdom."

"That is wondrous indeed, Master Alderton. Have you taken many captives?"

"Me? Nay, brother." The captain smiled. "The only prisoners I have taken are a few French hens, and they ended up in the cooking pot before the day was out."

Thomas beamed, happy that for once he had understood a joke.

"And what of archers who are taken prisoner? How much is their ransom?"

The laughter in Alderton's eyes turned in an instant to a menacing glare. For a brief moment, Thomas felt as if a weight pressed on his heart, making it difficult to breathe. Then the older man sighed.

"You are an innocent, brother," Alderton said. "A poor man cannot pay a ransom. An archer taken by the enemy can expect only a blade in the belly or a crushed skull."

Alderton's bleak words silenced Thomas.

"Well, brother, is your curiosity satisfied?" the captain asked.

"I am grateful for your wisdom and your patience, Master Alderton," the monk responded. "May I ask you a final question?"

"Ask away, brother," came the cheerful reply.

"You have explained a great deal about why men go to the wars, and yet for every man who goes there are a hundred who stay safe in England. Is there not some other reason that makes men leave their homes, and all they hold dear, to risk their lives?"

"You see much for a monk," said the archer. "'Tis true. Most men will fight if they have no choice or to protect their homes, but few willingly set out to risk their necks. Many who turn to soldiering are drawn by something in their blood, be it a craving for adventure, a love of fighting or some other restlessness. They have no wish to spend their days in the miserable hovels where they were born, staring at a horse's arse as they plough the same stony field season after season in return for a mouthful of bread. No, they want to see the world. They want to be a part of the stories of kings and wars rather than just listen to them around the winter fire. More than anything, they want to taste life before death shuts their eyes, and war is the greatest test for any man, whatever his station in life."

"Do they find what they seek?"

"Many find nothing except an early grave." Alderton paused, momentarily mulling over his own words. "There is nothing like war. It gets in your blood, and you can't settle down to anything else."

The archer abruptly stood. Thomas stumbled to his feet.

"I am in your debt, Master Alderton. You have taught me more about soldiers than all the books of the ancient commanders I have studied in our monastery's library," he said.

"Ah, of Alexander and Hannibal and other great captains." The archer laughed at the monk's surprise. "Aye, I am not completely unschooled. War is my chosen profession, brother Thomas, and many a night I have spent with other captains talking of such things."

Embarrassed by his frankness, Alderton gruffly pointed to the flask of brandy wine.

"Give that Cheshire captain a swig or two, and promise him the rest if he gives a true count of his men. He can speak proper English if he has a mind to it."

"Thank you," said Thomas, more for the rough kindness than the flask. "At times, it scarcely seems that the army comes from a single nation. Such a babble of tongues and dialects."

"They are all Englishmen of one type or another." The captain grinned. "Except for the Welsh. But those godless little bastards fight like devils, and it's better they're killing Frenchmen rather than knifing us."

And by such stratagems and ruses, a report was given to the king by the end of the day that the army which would march to Calais would number some six thousand men, of which one thousand or so would be men-at-arms and five thousand archers. Another fifteen hundred men were staying to garrison Harfleur, the barest minimum needed to give any hope that it would not fall back into the hands of the French as soon as the main English force marched out of sight.

The king gave no sign of his feelings when he heard the figures, the chief steward later told his underlings as he described the scene.

"Fighting and the leading of armies is a king's business, of course," sniffed the man after draining half the tankard of beer his deferential listeners had put in front of him. "But it seems precious few men to go marching across France with."

"And we march with them," one of the audience sombrely remarked.

"Aye," his chief agreed reluctantly as he sluiced down the last of the beer.

---

7 OCTOBER

The Royal Chancery 5:48 p.m.

Sir Gilbert Umfraville looked again at the chart held up by two servants. He glared at the nervous clerk of the royal household standing beside him.

"You call this a map?" he demanded.

"It is all we have, Sir Gilbert," the clerk replied. "It is said to be the best description of this area of France. It was compiled by the most learned men."

"Looks more like the depraved lusting of some lecherous monk," the knight retorted.

Of an old Norman family from Northumberland, Umfraville was only twenty-five, but almost half his life had been spent commanding men in war. He was a giant, more than six and a half feet tall with the muscular grace of a natural athlete; he could also out-think most men, whether it was at the council table or in the second it took to draw a sword. Umfraville had been given the task of planning the army's route to Calais.

No one in the English camp knew this part of France or had travelled the hundred and forty miles from Harfleur to Calais. The few Frenchmen willing to talk, either for pay or to see the back of the detested English, said it took eight days following the dirt track that was the nearest thing to a road. All of the informants were vague on what the English would meet on the way.

A search of Harfleur had yielded a map at the bottom of a chest in the mayor's house. It was a beautiful document, richly illustrated in blue and red ink with portraits of naked women and fat-bottomed cherubs in gold leaf around the edges. At its centre was a portrait of Harfleur, resembling a fairy kingdom.

"What's this?" Umfraville gestured at a little box containing a Latin inscription at the bottom of the sheet.

The clerk looked at the inscription, and frowned. "Ah, yes. Well," the man mumbled, nervously looking at his feet.

"What does it say? Do you think I can read and write? I am a nobleman, not a mincing pen-pusher," the knight barked.

"Um," the man stammered. "It appears to say the map is based on the lay of the land in the time of Julius Caesar, the ancient

Roman who first conquered the savage tribes of this area many centuries ago."

Umfraville uttered a mocking bark. "This thing is as useful as a map of Hell, because that's where it's likely to lead us."

"Your pardon, Sir Gilbert," the clerk pleaded. "I had not seen the inscription."

Umfraville motioned the man to silence with a flick of his hand.

"We know only the general direction to Calais. We don't know how long it will take to get there. We don't know what lies along the way. And we have only the ghost of some dead ancient to guide us," said the knight. "Well, it will have to do."

The clerk, thinking the knight was finished, bowed and reached to take the map from the servants.

"Stay your hand," Umfraville commanded. "I will keep this pretty nothing. It will make for an amusing story if I ever return home. Either that or I can wipe my arse on it."

The King's Tent, 10:02 p.m.

Henry listened as the priest intoned the sombre Latin verses of the service marking the end of the day. Two candles on the plain wooden altar flickered as the king knelt on the bare dirt floor of the tent.

> Lighten our darkness, we beseech thee, O Lord:
> and by thy great mercy defend us
> from all perils and dangers of this night.

The words seemed achingly sad to Henry, full of the frailty and pleading of mere mortals lost in the vast and dark cosmos. He listened to the words, hoping for a sign that Heaven was with him, but nothing came as the chant filled the tent.

> Abide with us, O Lord,
> for it is towards evening and the day is far spent.

Were his own days almost done? he wondered. Was he about to lead the army to disaster? He stared at the feeble flames of the candles, and then realised that the service was finished. Effortlessly, the king rose, crossed himself and turned. Nothing in his looks or manner suggested the doubts of a moment before.

"Your majesty," the waiting nobles greeted Henry. A final council had been called before the army departed the next day.

"My thanks for attending us, my lords." Men only ignored a royal summons if they were on their deathbed or in open rebellion, but the young ruler was faultless in his courtesy.

"The army's order of march is complete?"

"It is, sire," York confirmed.

"Good. You, cousin, will command the rearguard with the earl of Oxford."

York bowed in acknowledgement. There would be no dishonour in leading the rear of an army that was likely to be pursued across France by a larger force.

"And you valiant gentlemen shall lead the vanguard with joint authority." The king inclined his head to Sir John Cornwall and Sir Gilbert Umfraville. "Few armies are so fortunate as to be able to boast of experience such as yours. We, with our brother Gloucester, shall command the centre."

None of the lords and captains demurred. The king had listened to every argument and reason on why it was folly to march into the arms of the French with just six thousand men – and rejected them all.

Henry turned to a tall blue-eyed man standing slightly apart from the others. "And you, my lord, shall hold Harfleur for us."

The earl of Dorset, the newly appointed commander of the town, bowed. He did not look happy.

"How go the repairs?" Henry asked.

English masons and labourers had begun mending the holes torn in the town walls by the siege.

"Well enough, sire. Most of the work on the outer walls will be completed in a few days. Restoring the town itself will take many weeks, although that work is less urgent. There is ample room for our men now most of the populace has been expelled."

"Good." Henry's tone held no doubt about the order he had given to drive so many people from their homes.

"We have sent to London to recruit good English folk to come and settle here," the king continued. "Soon you will have many honest hands to aid you, Dorset. For now, you must make do with those you have. We have given you all the men we can spare."

"Thank you, sire. I hope it will be sufficient."

"Sufficient?" ironically replied the king. "A fifth of our army while we go to face the might of France?"

"Unless the might of France descends on us after your majesty and the army depart," Dorset stolidly replied.

"And if they do?"

"We shall hold them until they give up or we are overwhelmed."

"I have no doubt of that. But tell me, what is the mood of your men? Do they count themselves blessed or cursed to stay behind?"

"In truth, they cannot decide who faces the greater risk, sire. We who remain or those who march with you," the earl responded.

"Then they are wise, indeed, for such plain and humble fellows. Who but the Almighty knows who has drawn the more difficult lot."

It was clear from the expressions of the listening lords that the royal council was in complete agreement for once.

A squire bowed just within Henry's eyesight. With the slightest gesture of his hand, the king commanded the man to speak.

"Your majesty, the royal herald and the French knight have returned."

Some of the nobles looked half hopeful as de Gaucourt and the English herald who had taken Henry's challenge of single combat to the French were ushered into the tent.

"Greetings." The king acknowledged their bows. "You bring news?"

"We bring no answer to your challenge, sire," said the herald, a tall, reedy man.

"How so, herald?"

"We were not permitted to travel beyond Rouen, sire. Instead, we were detained there for several days despite my protestations that our lawful business was with the court in Paris."

"And our message to the French court?"

"It was taken to Paris by one of my French brethren, although I pointed out this was against all the rules of heraldry."

"And did the French herald bring back an answer."

A curt shake of the man's head was the only response.

"No matter. Silence can be as clear as a thousand words."

Henry turned to de Gaucourt, who had stood silent while the herald recounted the tale of their fruitless journey.

"You are welcome, sir. The answer, or the lack of one, is no fault of yours."

The French knight bowed.

"And what other tidings do you bring?" Henry turned back to the herald. A herald's role included gathering intelligence.

"A large French army is at Rouen."

"How many?" Henry asked.

"At least ten thousand. The French crown prince lies with a second force at Vernon, which is some eight days' march to the east of Calais. Reports suggest his army may be as large as the force in Rouen."

Several of the listening nobles paled under the dirt and grease that coated their unwashed faces; others mumbled or shook their heads. Even the most pessimistic had not imagined the enemy would raise such numbers.

"Are you saying there are twenty thousand French waiting for us?" blurted one.

"I can only be sure of what I saw at Rouen," the herald replied.

"What else did you see?" Henry calmly retook control of the questioning.

"The land between Harfleur and Rouen is alive with armed men, sire. I have never seen its like anywhere. It is as if the entire country is an ant heap come alive at the midsummer swarming."

Even Henry paused at the reply. "And you, de Gaucourt? What do you say?"

"It is true, sire. All of France is arming for war. Nobles whose families have hated each other for generations are embracing, and vowing to fight side by side. Peasants and townsmen who would normally never think of leaving the safety of their homes clamour to fight as loudly as the bravest knights. The rich are giving money to raise troops as if they were buying their way into Heaven. There is a mood in the country that none has ever seen before."

"And what is the cause of these wondrous things?"

"You, sire." De Gaucourt held Henry's gaze as he replied. "You have succeeded in uniting France in a way not seen in generations."

Henry smiled.

"Always you speak plainly," the king said. "It is a noble and all too rare quality." He turned to his commanders. "My lords, we should not be fearful. Do you not recall the great deeds of Edward III and his son, the Black Prince? Of how they rode across France with only a few men at their backs? And yet they won great victories at Crecy and Poitiers? Are we lesser men than they?"

Sir John Cornwall's Tent, 11:32 p.m.

Thomas was waiting when Sir John returned to his quarters from the royal council. The knight accepted the cup of wine offered by his squire; he was too tired, for once, to complain about its poor quality.

"So, monk, soon you will see more than you ever imagined when you decided to leave the safety of your cloisters," the older man wearily grunted.

The peculiar clinking sound made only by men clad in armour broke the silence outside the tent.

"Surely the Almighty will watch over us," Thomas replied uncertainly.

The knight, pondering what had happened in the king's tent, seemed not to hear. "Our king is a truly dangerous man," he said a moment later.

He raised a hand before the shocked monk could protest. "Henry is a good man and an even better king. But he is driven to prove himself before the only judge that matters to him."

"God?" Thomas asked.

"God. Fate. Destiny. Call it what you will. Henry will not stop until he triumphs. Either that or he meets his death. And Heaven help those of us who follow him."

PART II

THE MARCH TO THE SEA

English Camp, Harfleur, 6:38 a.m.

Trumpet calls and the beat of drums rose above the din of thousands of milling men and horses as the army formed up to march to Calais. Captains cursed and threatened as they chased their men into line; blows from leathered hands and boots hurried the slow and the lame. Pink-faced young lords and knights stood in little groups amid the chaos, boasting of how many Frenchmen they would kill in the coming days.

The army was glad to be turning its back on Harfleur and the English camp that reeked of pestilence and the pits where thousands of men had relieved themselves since summer. Thoughts of England and home filled the soldiers' heads. The men picked to stay behind to hold Harfleur glumly watched from the town's walls; their departing friends below barked quick farewells and hurried away, reluctant to meet their eyes.

Wagoners, grooms and stewards swarmed around the baggage train, making final checks. The wagons and carts contained just enough food for the eight days it was reckoned it would take the army to reach Calais, mostly dried meats and nuts. A handful of each were sufficient for a man to ride or march for a day, and have enough energy at the end of the day to complain of the piss-poor rations. Most of the rest of the space was taken up with the half a million arrows on which the army's fate would hang if it should encounter the French.

The army would march in a long straggling line of contingents of different size, ranging from the duke of Gloucester's company, with six knights, a hundred and ninety-three men-at-arms and six hundred archers, to the tiny band of Thomas Strickland, a poor squire of Cumbria with just two men-at-arms and six archers. To any passer-by it would resemble a gaggle of peasants trudging to market rather than a disciplined host. Men were schooled in their villages or lord's castle on how to fight with bow, sword or lance, but nothing more. Armies only came together for a month or two when there was a war – there was no time to drill the troops in anything more than forming a rough battle line. A few of the lords and monks had read with wonder in ancient texts of the legions of old Rome, of how ten thousand men moved and turned as one on a single command. Such skills had not been seen on the battlefields of Europe for a thousand years.

Before the King's Tent, 6:45 a.m.

Henry strode from his tent. He was clad in polished steel plate armour that glittered even in the grey October light. A red and blue linen surcoat decorated with the golden leopards of England and the lilies of France covered the breastplate. A war sword hung from a chain belt, and he held a helmet with a thin gold crown encircling the dome. Exchanging the helmet for the reins of a horse grasped by a squire, the king effortlessly hoisted himself into the saddle. Taking the helmet from the squire's upheld hands, the king placed it on his head before turning the horse with a tug of the bridle to face the waiting lords and captains.

"Begin," the king ordered the priest who had followed him from the tent.

With a bow, the man unrolled a parchment, and began to read in a loud, clear voice trained by years of chanting Church services.

"By the grace of God, Henry king of England and France, doth hereby charge and command that his army shall march this day to Calais. Moreover, the king commands that the army shall conduct itself in a lawful and peaceful manner so that his French subjects need have no fear for their lives or their lawful property."

The scribe read a list of commands for the army's conduct on the march. Soldiers were not to steal or loot; only such food as the army needed would be taken; any man caught stealing would pay with his life.

"The king commands that no woman may travel with the army or approach within three miles of the camp," the monk continued. "Any woman caught within the army's lines will be expelled and warned not to return. A woman who violates such an order, and is caught again, shall have her right arm broken."

Surprise and amusement rippled across the faces of some of the listening lords. A few shook their heads in disbelief at what they saw as the king's prudery.

"Finally," the reader concluded, "the king commands that no man, whether lord, common soldier or servant, shall blaspheme or swear. God and his saints must not be profaned or offended."

Rolling up the parchment, the cleric bowed to Henry, who dismissed him with a single word of thanks.

Lord Camoys inclined his head to the king; it was hard to tell if the old man's expression was ironic amusement or derision.

"Most novel orders, sire," he said. "Doubtless, it will be good to have the saints march at our side, although it will be a rare army where common soldiers do not swear. While I do not presume to speak for others, my own men can barely take breath without uttering lewd phrases. As for an army without whores, I doubt such a thing has ever been imagined before, let alone seen."

"We can but try, my lord." Henry calmly regarded the sardonic noble. "No man who flouts Heaven can hope to prevail, especially men whose business is war and killing. Those least of all."

"Sire!" Sir Gilbert Umfraville interjected. "Will you order the army to depart? Time passes quickly."

"With all my heart," the king replied in a voice that for once showed emotion. "Let us begin our great venture."

—— 10 OCTOBER ——

Rouen, Late Afternoon

An elderly man was sitting in the castle garden reading a prayer book when the messenger arrived. Sweat glistened on the rider's dirty face and his tangled black hair; he stank of hot leather and horse. Wordlessly, the exhausted man held out a leather cylinder.

Jean Boucicaut, marshal and captain general of the French army, carefully laid the prayer book on the stone bench before reaching for the tube. He extracted a sheet of parchment, and studied it.

"You rode all the way from Harfleur?" he asked the messenger a minute later.

The rider nodded.

"And you saw the English army?"

"As they left the town, my lord. Two days ago."

"This says they number some six thousand," the sitting man pointed at the parchment. "Do you agree?"

"We watched from a hilltop. They rode or marched two or three abreast. It was not difficult to make an accurate count."

"And they march for Calais?"

"That is the word from our spies in the town. The English made no secret of their destination."

"Six thousand. It is not very many, and they have far to go," the other mused. "This young English king appears to be either rash or witless."

"Our own army is many times larger, and reinforcements arrive every day from all over France," the rider said. "We will crush them."

"Yes, but it is better not to be too confident," Boucicaut replied.

Rising effortlessly, he called to a knight waiting nearby. "Mobilise the army. We march within the hour," he commanded.

─── 11 OCTOBER ───

Outside the Town of Arques

The English army marched for three days before encountering any resistance. The vanguard had just reached the banks of the Bethune River when a thunderbolt slammed into the murky water, sending up a column of spray and sludge that drenched every man within a hundred yards.

"Cannon!" A tall archer pointed at the castle on a hill above the town on the far side. A plume of white smoke rising from an embrasure confirmed his words.

"We cannot cross while that monster threatens us," Sir Gilbert Umfraville cursed.

"You –" he motioned to a rider – "take word to the king. Say the French stir at last." Turning to the advance guard, the knight ordered the men to move back into the trees along the riverbank. The order did not please them.

"Sir Gilbert, let us cross and kill these cowardly loons who fight with smoke and magic," called one of the archers.

"Worry not." The knight bared his yellow teeth in a wolfish grin. "You will have a bellyful of killing soon enough."

"Aye," called another man. "Against foes we can gut face-to-face."

For half a day the army waited, stalled on the wrong side of the river until an English herald returned from the castle. The message he had taken from Henry to its lord was succinct: yield or your castle and town will be burned, and you and your kinsmen hung from your own walls. The portly French lord surrendered without a word. A peace offering of six wagons loaded with bread and casks of wine was sent out to appease the English. Stewards took charge of the food, dispensing a share to each passing contingent as the army resumed the march.

"Not bad. Better with some meat," Umfraville grunted after finishing half a loaf. "Still, it will cheer the men, will it not, Master Feriby?"

John Feriby was the king's wagon master. He was a stout man in his forties with a balding head and a coarse black beard. It was his duty to feed the army and make sure the wagon train kept up with the fighting men. Feriby had years of experience; there were few men in Europe who could match his skill or cunning.

"Better if they had yielded ten times as much," the wagon master grumbled. "This lot won't fill many bellies."

"Always you worry," scoffed Umfraville, but his voice was kind. Even the bravest army needed supplies if it was to last a single day. Those who truly knew the art of war treated men such as Feriby with respect.

"What is it?" Umfraville's grin vanished as the wagon master suddenly bent double in the saddle. A gasp of pain escaped the older man's clenched teeth.

"Just my guts, Sir Gilbert," Feriby grunted a moment later. "No doubt it is this foul French fare."

"You must rest, good master" the young knight gently chided.

"Nay. What use is a wagon master on his back? It is nothing."

Umfraville suddenly realised that what he had taken as marks of weariness on Feriby's face were the first signs of the flux that had killed so many men. He said nothing. It was clear the wagon master knew he would be dead before many more days had passed. Until then he had duties to attend to.

— 12 OCTOBER —

Eu

The French did not yield so easily on the following day. Shortly after noon the army came in sight of a broad, muddy river. Scouts said it was called the Bresle, but to the soldiers it was just another unwelcome obstacle. A large grey stone castle guarded the town of Eu at the crossing point.

A force of French knights suddenly surged out of a thicket of trees and fell on the six English scouts who had crossed the river alone to reconnoitre the far bank. The scouts, clad only in leather and wool jerkins, were hacked from the saddle in swirling knots of flashing swords and screaming horses. One French knight, a hulking man in full armour, decapitated one of the English riders with a single sword cut, and then hewed off the arm of a second at the shoulder. The French casually surveyed the bodies of the butchered scouts before riding slowly back to the safety of the castle walls. English soldiers on the far bank could hear their laughter.

Once again Henry sent a herald to demand the town surrender or be stormed and all within the walls slaughtered. The hotheads in the garrison who wanted to fight were overruled by their timid elders. The town opened its gates, and wagons loaded with bread and wine were sent out to the English. Henry ignored those of his nobles who clamoured to linger in the town for a night, and sleep in comfortable beds. The king and his more experienced lieutenants knew there was no time to waste, and he ordered the army to march on.

On the March

Thomas rode beside Sir John Cornwall as the army marched away from Eu. They had barely spoken for two days. The knight's duties at the head of the army had left little time for more than passing greetings.

"We make good progress, do we not, Sir John?" the monk prompted. "Will we reach Calais soon?"

"Our scouts reckon we have covered half the distance, some eighty miles or so," Cornwall replied. "Some of them know their craft, so it may be true."

"Heaven be praised." The monk beamed.

"Their other news is less pleasing: the scouts report finding more and more signs of French cavalry every day. Packs of them have dogged our flanks for the past two days, and more are gathering in front of us."

Startled, Thomas glanced at the fields on either side of the track. All he could see was the same empty landscape dotted with patches of trees through which the army had marched since it left Harfleur.

Cornwall smiled. "God's teeth, lad. You won't see them. They stay out of sight, following us like wolves hunting their prey, watching for weaknesses."

The monk reddened with embarrassment; always he had to be the innocent fool.

"Will they attack?" he asked a moment later.

"As surely as God is in his Heaven," Cornwall replied as calmly as if they were talking of the likelihood of rain. The knight smiled at his companion's horrified expression. "Come, Thomas," he soothed. "You did not really imagine that we would march to Calais like fat pilgrims who wander along dreaming only of guzzling ale and pinching the serving wenches at the next inn?"

Sir John paused to bark at a detachment of archers slowing down the vanguard. The men were starting to feel the effects of the rapid pace the king was forcing. One of the men spat at the ground, muttering that fat-arsed knights should try walking. Knowing the men were tired, Cornwall ignored the insolence.

"The French are determined that we shall never see Calais," he resumed the conversation. "Still, Henry knows what is required if we are to reach safety."

"What is that, Sir John?" Thomas's dejection gave way to his customary curiosity.

"Discipline. Some say it is the deadliest weapon in warfare, and all too often the rarest. And it is likely to be the difference between finishing this journey or ending up dead under a hedge."

Cornwall's features lightened as he forgot the demands of command for a moment.

"Discipline is the difference between an armed mob and an army. A mob can lay waste to an entire country like a plague of devils. No man's gold or woman's virtue is safe. And yet that is the point. Men without discipline, no matter how brave or handy with a blade, are just a rabble. They are not an army that can stand and fight."

The knight thought for a moment, searching for the right words.

"Discipline binds an army together like steel, and makes it fight as one; it multiplies its strength many times over. An army will defeat a mob that is ten or even a hundred times its size," Cornwall explained. "Henry understands all of this. More importantly, he knows how to instil discipline. Very few men have such a gift."

Thomas waited, but the knight said nothing more.

"Do the French not have discipline, also?" he finally ventured.

The knight slowly turned his great bearded head and gazed at the monk.

"I hope not, Thomas," he answered. "I truly hope not."

—— 13 OCTOBER ——

Blanchetaque

"Kneel, you French swine!" barked the English sergeant as he and a second man-at-arms forced the struggling prisoner to his knees. The order was followed by a stinging cuff from the sergeant's fist. Blood trickled from the cut it left on the captive's lip.

"Enough, good fellows. Leave him," Henry called from his horse. The Frenchman had been brought to the king for questioning. The men-at-arms hesitated.

"Fear not," Henry assured them. "He will do us no harm."

The soldiers reluctantly stood back.

"An enemy scout, sire," gruffly explained the sergeant. "We took him by ambush in yonder woods. He and his friends were trailing the army."

Six days of marching had brought the English army within sight of the Somme River, the last major obstacle before Calais.

"Fellow," Henry addressed the man in French. "What is your name, and whence come you?"

The prisoner was momentarily startled at the sudden switch to his own language. He had understood nothing of what had been said until that moment. "It is I who should ask what is your name that you dare to march across France with this rabble of cutthroats and whoremongers!" the man shot back.

The members of Henry's entourage who spoke enough French to understand the captive's outburst gasped or looked shocked. The sergeant, who had not understood a word, raised his hand to strike the prisoner again.

Henry stilled them all with a gesture.

"Pay no heed," he said soothingly in English. "We should not fear high spirits."

Turning to the prisoner he lapsed into French. "A fair question if rudely put. I am Henry of England and France, and your rightful king. So I say again, what is your name and whence come you?"

The reply disconcerted the scout. He had taken Henry in his simple grey wool tunic for a captain or a knight at most. "You are Henry?" he asked doubtfully. "King Henry?"

"Indeed. And who are you, good sir?"

"I am Jean, a servant of Marshal Boucicaut, who will soon be the instrument of your destruction, and of these fools and scoundrels who follow you." The man had quickly recovered his nerve.

"He says he is a servant of Marshal Boucicaut, the commander of the French army," the king explained to those who had not understood the exchange. "Boucicaut is a warrior and leader of great renown."

"If this dog speaks true we may assume the master is not far off," the duke of York said.

The ensuing silence was broken by the prisoner; sensing that his revelation had unsettled the English, he taunted them. "This is an ill day for England," he asserted. "My master waits for you at the river with six thousand knights and men-at-arms. The crossing is barred with great stakes. You will be cut to pieces."

Henry listened impassively. His calm gaze appeared to discomfort the prisoner.

"Brave words," the king finally said. "Do you speak the truth or merely make empty boasts?"

"It is true," the enemy scout retorted.

"Hear me. If you are lying, your head shall not sit on your shoulders for another day."

"I speak the truth," the man shot back. "You need only go another a mile or two up the road to see for yourself."

Henry beckoned to the two men-at-arms. "See no harm comes to him until we decide his fate," he commanded.

"I speak the truth. Go and see for yourself, Henry of England!" the prisoner shouted as he was led away.

"What shall we make of these tidings, Sir John?" the king asked Cornwall.

"It is doubtless true, sire. The French could hardly pick a better place. Our men will be badly exposed if we try to cross the river. It is broad, and even a small defending force will inflict grievous losses. And if the French are as many as that varlet claims, it will be a bloodbath."

"What then are our options?" the king asked his commanders.

Lord Camoys answered with his usual sour smile.

"This ford is the last before the coast, sire. After this the scouts say the river is too wide and swift to cross as it approaches the sea. Finding another crossing will mean following the river eastwards, deeper into France and away from Calais and our ships. The French will pursue us, and their numbers will only grow. If we do not find another crossing, we shall be trapped."

"Always the flinty voice of reality, my lord," Henry said. He thought for a moment. "We have three choices: we turn back to Harfleur, we attempt to cross here or we march inland in hope of finding another crossing." He added, "We need not waste time considering the first option. There will be no going back."

All of the lords nodded. Henry could see the agreement was sincere; the French would only pursue them, and the army would end up trapped in Harfleur with no hope of rescue.

Cornwall pushed his horse a step ahead of the other commanders.

"I will lead the attack if you decide to cross the river here, sire, but I urge you not to," he said.

"You would have us refuse to fight?"

"If we are to fight it is better to do so on a ground of our choosing," the knight said.

"So we march into the lion's den?" Henry tossed the question out to the men arrayed in front of him.

It was met with silence. Seeing the uneasiness and doubt in his lieutenants' faces, Henry gazed towards the river where he knew that the French were waiting unseen.

"Time is not on our side. Our supplies will only last another two or three days, and the French are closing in on us. To cross the river here would be best, but success is not assured. And I have no wish to turn the river red with the blood of hundreds of our men. The alternative then is to march inland in search of an unguarded crossing, and hope we do not encounter the main French army. Does that sum it up?" he asked.

"As always, sire." York spoke for all of them.

"Then we will march east," Henry said, "and hope that fortune favours us."

The impromptu council broke up without another word.

"Stay a moment," Henry ordered Cornwall. "What of the army's mood, old friend?" he asked when the two men were alone.

"There's some grumbling. Nothing serious."

"All is well, then?"

"No, you know it is not, lad," Cornwall answered with the familiarity the king allowed him in the most private moments.

"Soldiers can cope with most things: tired feet, hungry bellies, empty beer barrels. It's uncertainty and doubt that undoes an army. Most of the men set out on what they thought would be an easy march to Calais. Now they're not so sure, and some already begin to wonder if they will ever see England again."

The French waiting at the river heard the English trumpets ordering the retreat. Five thousand armour-clad men were drawn up on foot in tight lines facing the crossing; hundreds of crossbowmen lined the riverbank, ready to mow down the English.

"They are not coming," said Marshal Boucicaut as he listened to the distant call of the trumpets. "They will march inland in hope of finding another way."

"Do we attack?" his lieutenant asked. "We almost match their numbers, and they will be tired."

"No need," the older man replied calmly.

"But they will get away," his companion protested.

"How?" Boucicaut said. "They are marching straight towards our main army."

--- 16 OCTOBER ---

Boves

The English army marched away from the sea, moving deeper and deeper into France. Every crossing of the Somme was blocked. Patrols returned to say that the bridges at Pont Remy and Abbeville were wrecked, and large French forces waited on the other bank. Henry listened silently to the glum reports, and ordered the march to continue. The food in the wagons had almost run out; rations were reduced to a handful of raw grain for each man. The army's mood blackened a little more each day.

Three Miles beyond Boves, 3:07 p.m.

The land was deserted, every village and farmstead abandoned. Hungry English soldiers searching for food found each dwelling stripped bare; anything that could not be carted or carried away by the French had been burned or fouled with excrement.

"Why do the French hang these red rags on their dwellings?" an archer asked his companion.

There were seven cottages in the hamlet; strips of dirty red cloth were nailed to the door of each one. The two men had just emerged from one of the hovels.

"'Tis bad news for the likes of us, William" said a third man as he approached.

John Hampton and William Mason smiled at the newcomer.

"Master Alderton," each said respectfully.

"Good morrow, lads," the captain greeted his two sergeants. Hampton was the older of the two, a flinty-faced man with thinning ginger hair and piercing eyes that regarded the world suspiciously. Mason was his opposite, smiling and friendly with a thatch of badly cut yellow hair and sunny blue eyes.

Alderton tore the red rag from the door.

"What does it mean, captain?" Mason asked.

"In times of great peril the French army raise a red flag," Alderton said.

"Is it the banner of their king?"

"No. It is a sign that they will take no prisoners. Any man they capture will be killed on the spot. And now the French peasants imitate their godless masters with these rags to taunt us."

"Truly?" said the younger man. "They will show no quarter?"

"Aye, lad."

Hampton snorted derisively. "No need of a special flag. The likes of us have never been shown mercy by the French."

"True enough." Alderton tossed the red rag on the ground.

"Forget all those stories of glory and chivalry you heard at home, William," the captain said. "Any common soldier taken in battle can expect only to have his throat slit or his head broken."

"The French never take prisoners?" the young archer asked.

"Oh, they take prisoners. As long as they be lords and barons and the like. They get out of bed in the morning in hope of taking such captives. Rich men whom they can hold for fat ransoms. Or even a penniless knight is worth taking in their eyes: what he may lack in treasure is made up for by capturing a fellow warrior. It adds lustre to a gentleman's reputation. But there's no profit or merit for them in taking common men," Alderton continued coldly.

"And that's not the half of it," interjected Hampton.

"Aye, John. Tell him." Alderton nodded at the young archer.

"The French hate us more than any other kind," Hampton began.

"What? We English?" blurted Mason.

"Archers, you pig's bladder. The French hate us almost more than anything else on a battlefield except perhaps for the heathen Moors in the Holy Land," Hampton said.

"'Tis true," Alderton agreed. "They would have a special place in Hell reserved for the bowmen of England."

"Why?" said Mason. "How should we merit such hatred?"

"No man wants to die, but if a knight must perish in battle they think there is at least honour in falling at the hands of their own kind. They deem it an abomination to be struck down by what they regard as a peasant or beggar conceived in a quick tumble in a back alley," Alderton answered.

"Captain Alderton's words meet the mark as surely as his arrows," Hampton said. "The French show no mercy to any English archer who falls into their hands. And that's not the worst of it."

"How so?" the younger man paled.

"Some times the French take captured archers and hack off their hands and blind them rather than kill them. 'Tis their idea of justice," Hampton told him.

"Surely the king and his lords will guard us from such a fate if the army is beaten?" Mason looked hopefully at the two older men.

"They'll be too busy looking after their own skins, renewing old acquaintances with their French cousins and the like. Lords stick together." Hampton snorted. He glanced at the captain, suddenly sensing he had gone too far. "No offence, Master Alderton."

"You speak no less than the truth, John. Our gentlemen may need us in battle. Indeed, we may save their hides, and do most of the fighting and the dying. But once the battle is done they'd rather sup with their own kind, be they English or French." Alderton's eyes went to Mason. "William, hear me," he said softly. "Any man who goes to the wars courts a terrible death. The only true honour is to master your fear, and fight. If you can do that you are as good as any lord."

—— **17 OCTOBER** ——

Boves

There was no talk of honour when they hung the archer the next day. The bowman, a small, swarthy man, struggled and pleaded for mercy in a whiny London accent as he was dragged to a large elm tree by two guards. A grimy rope taken from the back of a cart had been knotted into a rough noose and tossed over a bare branch. A priest in a black habit trudged behind the struggling prisoner, reading aloud from a prayer book. The cleric rushed through the rites; his resentful tone made it clear he did not regard this as a worthy use of his time.

Henry and some household knights watched from their horses. The king's bare head was wet from the rain that had been falling from the ashen sky since dawn; his face was rigid with anger. Some two hundred archers stood in four ranks facing the tree; they would tell the rest of the army of what they were about to witness.

"Pardon his sins if it pleases you, oh Lord. Show mercy to his soul. Amen," the priest hurried through the final passage. Snapping shut the prayer book, he cursed audibly and dashed to a covered wagon.

A loud wail escaped from the archer as one of the guards looped the noose over his head and yanked it tight. A burly carter grasped the other end of the rope in hands as big as ham hocks.

Henry raised his right arm. Every eye, including those of the condemned man, were fixed on the upraised fist. Even the birds that had been watching from the treetops fell silent. A moment later the king's arm dropped, and the carter heaved on the rope. The archer shrieked as he shot six feet into the air; he went rigid for a fleeting second, and then his body convulsed as his legs thrashed wildly in the empty air. Agonised gasps escaped the man's lips as the thick rope cut into the bare throat; his face turned a deep red and then blackish purple as he slowly choked. The carter tied the end of the rope to the axle of his wagon.

Henry watched until the dangling man's crazed dancing slowed and then stopped. A moment later the king spurred his horse forwards to address the silent archers.

"This knave desecrated God's house and brought dishonour on us all. Know this! Blasphemy will not be tolerated. Our cause cannot triumph if we sin against Heaven."

Some of the archers hung their heads as the words lashed their ranks. Others stared stonily at the corpse dangling from the branch.

Henry could not tell from the archers' fixed expressions if they resented the hanging of one of their own or feared that the man's crime would bring God's wrath on their own heads. Hopes of French booty, after all, was one of the reasons they had left their homes to follow him. With a last look at the soldiers' sullen faces, the king nodded to the captains to march the men away. At that moment he noticed Sir John Cornwall and the young monk who was often at the old knight's side.

"Well, Sir John," he bitterly asked, "was it well done?" Distaste and a touch of self-mockery mingled in Henry's voice.

"Such things are necessary, sire," Cornwall replied. "An army is not a choir of angels."

"Can they not see that men who risk their lives on the battlefield should be the last to risk offending God?" There was a note of pained anguish in the question, but the king spurred his horse, and cantered off before the knight could answer.

Sir John saw Thomas's puzzlement.

"The wretch stole a communion dish from a church. It was worthless, a mere copper vessel, but it glittered brightly on the altar, and the fool in his greed imagined it was gold. The French priest came to our camp and demanded to see the king. In any other army he would have got a boot up his arse. But the guards know the temper of our Harry, and he was taken to the royal tent. I have rarely seen him so angry. He stormed up and down, furious that any man would not only break his orders, but rob a church. An immediate search was ordered. The archer could have tossed it in the bushes, but the simpleton tried to hide it in his sleeve. And now he has paid the price. And all for a copper pot not worth pissing in."

Thomas flinched at the knight's words.

"And the further we march the tighter the grip the king must keep on the army," the knight grimly added. "What happened yesterday could have been a disaster."

63

A French castle had surrendered the day before after Henry gave its master the choice of opening the gates or being stormed. The storerooms were almost empty of food, but some English soldiers discovered a large store of wine. Within minutes many were drunk.

"We came close to a mutiny when the king ordered the wine destroyed. Some of the men's swords were half out of their sheaths, and the archers reaching for arrows when Henry rode up. You should have seen it. He didn't say a word, just put himself between the wine and them. They slunk away like whipped dogs. Still, it was a near thing," Cornwall said.

The last of the archers had marched out of sight. The carter released the dangling body; it landed on the fallen leaves with a dull thud. He spat on the corpse, angry that he had been ordered to bury it.

Corbie

The French horsemen slammed into the English archers at full gallop. The wall of charging riders rode over the bowmen, hacking at their unprotected heads and chests with swords. A terrified archer sprawling on his back gaped mutely as a horse reared over him; a moment later the animal's descending iron-rimmed hooves burst the man's head like an overripe strawberry.

King Henry had decided to bypass the fortified town of Corbie rather than lose time demanding its surrender. The vanguard of the English army had passed by on the road skirting the town's main gate when a score of French men-at-arms charged out and attacked a contingent of archers that had fallen behind the rest of the column. Weary and half asleep, the bowmen barely grasped what was happening before the French were in the middle of them, slashing and stabbing at the stunned men's unprotected heads and chests.

A French knight tore down on a boy holding a flag. The youth, who looked no more than twelve, stood transfixed, staring open-mouthed at the thunderbolt of armoured flesh; he made no attempt to run or reach to his belt for the small knife that was his only weapon. A second later the horseman split the boy's face from the forehead to the chin with a single sword slash and snatched the flag with his other hand. The knight brandished the banner as his mount danced on the dying child.

The other riders cheered, clustering around the knight to admire the white and blue standard with its image of a golden bear. The French turned and began riding back to the open gate. Scores of soldiers and civilians on the town walls cheered and clapped; three noble ladies waved white handkerchiefs at the beaming horsemen.

At that moment Henry and his retinue came into sight at the head of the main part of the army. One of the French riders saw a badly wounded English archer trying to crawl away; he leaned down and casually speared the man between the shoulders. The archer screamed with agony before collapsing face down in the dirt. Yanking his lance from the twitching body, the rider contemptuously shook it at the king. His companions laughed and hooted.

Henry, his face white with fury, pointed at the smirking spearman.

"Who will restore our honour?" he demanded.

Most of the men around Henry were too busy trying to see what was happening to react; others had drawn their swords to form a protective ring around the king.

John Bromley, a Yorkshire squire, was the first to respond to Henry's cry. Spurring his horse, he tore towards the French, his sword thrust out like a lance.

Some of the French men-at-arms laughed; one said the lone Englishman must be mad. Then they saw more riders behind Bromley. Half of the French turned their horses to meet the English; the others glanced nervously at the gate behind them.

"Fight!" bellowed the French knight, shaking the captured banner at those starting to edge towards the shelter of the walls.

Bromley smashed into the French horsemen a second later. His sword caught an enemy rider on the shoulder: he yanked the blade free from the half-severed bone in time to parry a blow. Three more English riders slammed into the confused, milling group. One speared a Frenchman in the chest.

"Come back!" screamed the French leader as some of his men turned and dashed towards the gate. The two great wooden doors were swinging together; the soldiers and townsfolk who had been cheering on the walls a moment before had vanished.

Bromley turned on the French leader. The knight struggled to hold his horse's reins and the flag as he parried the Englishman's sword cuts. Bromley hacked at the man's armoured head and shoulders as if he were cutting down a tree. With a scream, the knight lost his balance, toppled backwards and fell. Bromley leaned down and tore the banner from the man's grasp. What was left of the French force bolted. The last rider shot through the gates as they clamped shut.

"Good Master Bromley. You have done well. Our thanks." Henry accepted the rescued banner from the upheld hands of the kneeling squire. A long smear of blood reddened the white silk.

"The thanks are also to those who rode with me, sire," Bromley answered simply.

Henry smiled with pride and pleasure at the squire's modesty. "Then they too have our thanks. And in the right time, you and they shall have a more substantial reward," the king answered.

"For now, take this banner and restore it to those who lost it, so they might learn from your bravery." He motioned the squire to stand and handed back the flag.

The king looked up at the battlements. His brow knotted as he turned to study the lines of English soldiers marching along the road. York and the other lords waited for him to speak.

"This was nothing. A mere pinprick," Henry said after a moment. "But we must expect more attacks. And bigger ones."

There was silence as the king pondered for a few moments more.

"My lords, the army is stretched out over several miles. A thin line no more than three or four men wide at any point. We may be attacked at any moment by a French force lurking in the woods or some other place. Our men would be cut to pieces like a ribbon under a lady's scissors." The king looked at his council. "Every archer is to fashion a wooden stake. It shall be six feet long and sharpened at both ends. This is so it may be driven into the ground and also pierce a charging horse or its rider. If we are attacked the stakes can be erected to serve as a wall from behind which the archers will engage the enemy."

Henry dismissed them with a nod. He took the reins of his horse from a guard, and mounted. York and Gloucester cantered after the king.

"A curious stratagem." Camoys's tone conveyed curiosity rather than irony as he rode next to Sir Thomas Erpingham.

"It may well be useful," replied the knight.

"Have you experience of such a thing?" Camoys enquired.

"No, although I have heard its like before."

"Indeed?" Camoys was intrigued.

"It was used when the French fought against the Turks at the great battle of Nicopolis in the year 1396. The Christian knights charged the Turks and drove them back. But the Turks had erected a hedge of stakes with their archers drawn up behind them, and it broke the French charge. The Turks then slaughtered the French. It was a terrible day for Christendom," Erpingham explained.

"Most interesting," Camoys said. "Tell me, though, my lord: do you think such a trick can succeed twice?"

"It does no harm to try."

"Indeed. And the stakes can serve as crosses for our graves if it does not work," Camoys smiled.

—— 18 OCTOBER ——

Nesle

Finally, the scouts discovered an unguarded ford close to the hamlet of Nesle. There was no sign of the French. Henry decided the army would rest that night on the south bank of the river, and cross at dawn. He issued orders for the archers to practise with their bows as long as daylight remained.

"You are well, de Gaucourt?" Henry greeted the French knight. The king was standing on a small grassy mound overlooking a meadow where hundreds of bowmen in long lines were shooting at straw butts. Each volley cut through the air like a wind that springs up without warning on a spring day.

"I have no complaints." De Gaucourt bowed to the king.

"A wise policy for a prisoner, no doubt." Henry smiled briefly.

"It is still true, sire. Noble lords and knights welcome me at their firesides, and I share the same fare as the rest of the army," the Frenchman replied.

"Which is little enough. Still, we may hope for better things. I cross the Somme on the morrow. We shall soon reach Calais."

"It will still be many days' march to the sea. And you are likely to be detained along the way," de Gaucourt countered.

"What think you of the mood of our army?" Henry smiled again as the question visibly surprised the Frenchman.

"It is not my place to say," de Gaucourt responded guardedly.

"It is an honest question. A king must seek council."

"Even from his enemies?" De Gaucourt was still wary.

"From any man who has the wits and experience to judge a situation."

"Your pardon, sire. You have always shown me kindness. I should have realised you were not toying with me."

"I have little patience at the best of times for games."

"Then I will answer you frankly. The mood of your army changes like the seasons. The summer of your victory at Harfleur is a distant memory. Now there are only the bleak skies of autumn and the rain that drives away hope. Soon it will be winter, when those without food and shelter must die a cruel death in the cold."

"It seems you are a poet whose words are as sharp as the cut of your sword," the king said.

"Such afflictions as bad weather and empty bellies will seem like nothing when you meet the French army," de Gaucourt replied.

"In that case we shall fly home."

"Sire?" De Gaucourt seemed momentarily startled. "How?"

"With the aid of English yew wood and goose feathers."

Several of the king's companions laughed at the Frenchman's bewildered look.

"Good sir, fear not. I do not talk of sorcery," the king soothed. "There. That is how we shall return to our homes."

He pointed at the long line of bowmen. At that moment a captain shouted an order, and another volley of arrows arced into the sky.

"By the power of the longbow. It will overcome any challenge we may meet," Henry explained.

"True, it is a weapon with a fearful reputation. But what use will it be against a great army of armoured knights?" de Gaucourt said.

"The longbow has vanquished French armies in the past. It will again," interjected one of the king's companions.

"You speak of the battles of Crecy and Poitiers. I cannot deny that France suffered grievous defeats on those days. But that was long ago. Do you think we French have learned nothing since? And besides, your army is small, and its spirit is failing," the Frenchman stiffly replied.

Henry called to three archers standing guard nearby.

"Good Master Selby, I beg your aid," the king said to the eldest.

"This is John Selby, de Gaucourt. He is captain of one of my own companies of bowmen. He is a better archer than most of his men, but not so much better," Henry said. He turned to the archer, a tall man with deep hazel eyes and the ruddy complexion of most of the English bowmen. "Is that not true, John?"

"True enough, sire," the archer answered. "Every man in your royal companies has the skill of a master bowman. Else they would not be fit to serve in the ranks."

Selby was from Lancashire, and had been in the royal service for two decades. He was a dour man who drilled his men relentlessly in his determination to lead the best company in the army.

"Tell our French guest the secret of the English archer," Henry instructed.

"Years. Years of hard practice, that is," Selby answered. "Practice until the bow is as much a part of a man as his own right arm. A good archer fires ten to fifteen arrows in a minute on the battlefield. And each shaft will hit the target whether it be three hundred yards or three yards distant."

"Here, John," the king commanded. "Your bow."

Wordlessly, the man handed Henry the stave. It was six feet long and thick enough at the centre to fill a man's clenched fist. Henry proffered the unstrung weapon to de Gaucourt.

"You have skill with the bow?"

De Gaucourt took it. "In the hunt, of course. It is not a gentleman's weapon for war."

"No? Well, it is an Englishman's weapon." Henry's reply brought chuckles from the archers and the nobles.

"Here. Try it." Henry nodded at the bow.

Shrugging, the Frenchman fixed the bottom of the stave against his leg and tried to bend it so that he could loop the string over the top notch. He was shocked at the strength of the wood. There was more good-natured laughter as he struggled to string the bow. It took three attempts.

"What think you, John?" Henry asked Selby. "Has he the makings of an archer?"

"Better he stick to dancing with fine ladies and such like," the archer said.

De Gaucourt reddened at being mocked by a commoner.

"John is a stern taskmaster. You should not take his words unkindly," the king said. "Here. Try a shot." Henry handed de Gaucourt a yard-long arrow. De Gaucourt's eyes fixed on the razor-sharp steel head, and then at Henry standing unprotected just inches away. A single thrust and the English monarch would die. Some of the king's companions shifted uneasily; one or two reached for the hilts of their swords. Henry calmly returned the French knight's gaze.

"You are no murderer, my friend," Henry said.

De Gaucourt turned and raised the bow. Planting his feet as he had seen the English bowmen do, he began to pull on the string. It came back only halfway. He pulled at the string with all of his strength, grunting with the effort, but it moved only a few more inches. A spasm of anger reddened his face: he jerked savagely at the string. As if it was a living thing, the twine bit into his unprotected fingers and snapped back.

Henry placed a hand on de Gaucourt's shoulder, holding out the other for the bow. The Frenchman shrugged and handed the weapon to him. Henry took it and nocked an arrow. And then, with a single fluid movement, he thrust the bow forwards with his outstretched left arm as his right pulled the string back, using the full strength of his shoulders and torso. A split moment later the arrow was hundreds of yards away, sailing towards the distant line of trees.

"What think you, John?" Henry asked Selby.

"Not bad, sire. With practice you might get a place as a boy recruit. Mind, you'd have to work hard," came the reply.

De Gaucourt was stunned at the man's effrontery, but the king and his companions only laughed. Henry inspected the bow.

"You know, de Gaucourt, to pull a great warbow is the same as lifting a hundred pounds of iron with a single hand," Henry explained.

"True, sire," Selby confirmed. "But that's only the start. In battle an archer must draw that weight many times in a single minute. That is the true challenge. It is work that would break the back of untrained men."

Silence followed the captain's words.

De Gaucourt was deep in thought as he followed the royal party from the field.

"Why so glum?" asked Sir Walter Hungerford, walking beside him. The two men had become affable companions, sitting and talking by the campfire at night.

"I have not seen a king mingle with common men. Or use a bow other than for the hunt. It is not fitting," the Frenchman replied.

"Our laws require that every man and boy whatever his rank must practise archery at least once a week. Indeed, other pastimes such as playing with balls or cock fighting are forbidden so they do not distract our youngsters," Hungerford explained. "Our boys start at seven or eight years to learn the bow. The king was put to it like every other youth."

"Was it King Henry who made this remarkable law?" de Gaucourt sourly asked.

Hungerford ignored his companion's tart tone. "Nay. It was the act of blessed King Edward. The victor of Crecy."

De Gaucourt winced at yet another mention of the great French defeat.

"That was long ago. Much has changed since then. Your common bowmen will not be able to withstand the chivalry of France now. It is always the quality of a man that counts in war. His spirit, and his breeding. Peasants cannot stand against knights and lords." De Gaucourt's voice was steely with conviction.

"I am a gentleman, I hope," Hungerford said. "I have seen several wars, and served with some of the finest warriors in Europe. And yet I would rather face a charge of the greatest knights in Christendom than go up against a band of English bowmen."

De Gaucourt snorted with disbelief.

"Nay, sir. I speak true." Hungerford shook his head. "I have seen an arrow fired by a good archer pierce four inches of the strongest oak. Mere iron armour cannot withstand the longbow, and even the best steel plate is not always strong enough."

He paused before adding, "You have not seen how massed archers can cut an army to pieces in mere minutes."

"Peasants do not have the courage to withstand cavalry. They will run," de Gaucourt doggedly insisted.

"There is no need. As you have just heard, a good archer can fire ten arrows a minute. The best will fire fifteen. Against that, no force on earth can come close let alone survive," the Englishman said.

"True bravery is when men of noble birth meet on the field of honour, not when a herd of unwashed peasants pepper their betters from afar with a coward's weapon." De Gaucourt choked off his angry torrent of words. "Your pardon, sir," he said stiffly. "I would not offend you."

Hungerford accepted the apology with a nod, and the talk turned to other things as the two men walked back to the camp.

—— **19 OCTOBER** ——

Bethencourt, 5:09 a.m.

"All is ready?" Henry asked Cornwall and Umfraville as the three men stood on the riverbank. The sun would not rise for another hour: they could barely make out the line of trees marking the other side.

"Aye, sire," Cornwall answered. "A contingent of archers will cross and secure the far side. Sir Gilbert and I will then lead the mounted vanguard across. The army will follow as soon as the crossing is secure."

A hundred archers waited at the ford. The black water looked treacherous as it raced past. Scouts who had crossed during the night had reported that the water was no higher than a man's waist, but none of the bowmen looked happy as they eyed the water; it was more than three hundred feet across.

"No sign of the French?" Henry again peered at the murk on the far bank.

"The scouts found nothing," Cornwall said. "It seems quiet."

Henry took a final look. He could see nothing. "I shall remain here while the army crosses," he said.

Henry saw Cornwall's apprehension. It would not be a safe place if the vanguard was marching into a trap; a hail of French crossbow bolts could rip out of the darkness without warning.

"No one else can best ensure that the army crosses swiftly, and in good order." Henry's tone was adamant.

"And none of our lords will dawdle or waste time arguing over who goes first," added Umfraville.

Cornwall reluctantly nodded agreement. Turning, he called softly to the captain of the waiting archers.

"Take your men across, Master Selby," he said.

Selby stepped into the swirling river; with only one step the water circled around his knees. His men followed in a single line. The archers slowly picked their way, fighting for balance as the water buffeted their thighs and then surged around their waists. One man slipped, and was swept away without a sound.

Selby stopped in the middle, holding up his hand for the file to halt as he looked for movement on the nearby bank. Satisfied, he signalled the column to move. Moments later, the archers swarmed up the bank, grateful to be on land again.

In the first grey smudge of dawn, Henry could see the silhouettes of the archers fanning out. Nothing seemed amiss as the bowmen formed a protective cordon.

"Begin the crossing," he commanded.

Cornwall and Umfraville spurred their reluctant horses into the water. A column of knights and men-at-arms followed. The animals snorted nervously as the water swirled around their legs; some of them stumbled on the rocky riverbed.

*   *   *

"Beware! The French!"

The cry came from an English archer on the far bank as a wave of horsemen exploded from the nearby trees. There were at least fifty riders. All were clad in full plate armour and mounted on hulking chargers bigger than the largest plough horse.

Lowering their lances, the French charged. In seconds they had covered half of the distance to the English line before most of the bowmen grasped what was happening. Some of the archers stumbled back a step or two, glancing over their shoulders at the ford, torn between standing and running. Every man had nocked an arrow as he stepped out of the water, and that now saved them.

"Aim low!" Selby had time to scream before a ragged volley of arrows shot out from the thin English line. Half of the arrows hissed harmlessly over the oncoming horsemen, others bounced off the armoured riders, but some of the needle-sharp tips slammed into the throats and chests of the horses. The stricken steeds somersaulted head-first; their riders were crushed beneath the animals or flung into the air before slamming to the ground.

A third of the enemy horsemen had been killed or knocked from the saddle, but the survivors were just twenty yards away as the bowmen frantically nocked a second arrow. A few of the archers managed to bring down a rider with hastily fired shots, but the range was too close and time too short to get off a full volley. Three archers hurled down their bows and dashed towards the river; the rest unsheathed swords or knives. None of the archers wore armour or helmets.

The French horsemen howled with triumph as they tore into the ragged English line. At least a dozen archers were impaled on French lances. With a half-ton or more of galloping horse and armoured man behind them, the lances shot through the archers' chests, exploding out of their backs in eruptions of blood, broken bone and torn flesh. One archer was decapitated when a lance caught him in the throat; the severed head shot into the air; the man's dying brain momentarily glimpsed his body below as it crumpled to the ground.

The bowmen fought back as best they could. Three pulled a knight from his horse. Another rider, seeing what had happened, slashed at the archers with a battle axe; the steel edge sliced through one man's skull, severing the face to the chin.

Half of the bowmen were dead or wounded. The survivors stood back to back in little groups, trying to parry and dodge the swinging swords and lance thrusts of the encircling horsemen. The French were too intent on massacring their defenceless prey to notice the English horsemen emerge from the ford, and charge. Many of the French were knocked from their saddles before they grasped what was happening. Only a few managed to fight back. A moment later the surviving Frenchmen were dashing for the woods, pursued by the English cavalry as the archers cheered and screamed insults at the backs of the fleeing enemy.

"God's teeth! That should never have happened." Cornwall's tone made it clear he blamed himself for the carnage. Scores of English and French bodies littered the ground; a horse wandered slowly amid them, searching for its fallen rider.

"The enemy must have crept up after our scouts made the last reconnaissance," Umfraville replied. "They grow bolder."

"At least they won't stop us getting across the river," Cornwall said. "Now we can march towards Calais instead of away from it."

"Aye, although we have at least a hundred miles more to go. This skirmish was nothing to what I fear is coming."

"If any man can lead this army to the sea, it will be him. Look." Cornwall pointed across the river.

Henry stood alone on the other bank as the army streamed over the crossing. He called out encouragement and praise as the soldiers passed within a few feet. Each man felt as if the king's eyes were on him. Proudly, they raised their heads and squared their shoulders, briefly forgetting their weariness and the uncertainty that lay ahead.

Near Bethencourt, 9:43 a.m.

"You be too late, brother. These poor lads is dead," said the archer guarding a row of blanket-shrouded corpses."

Thomas had been called to give the last rites to men cut down in the clash at the river crossing, but it had taken him an hour to find the makeshift infirmary set up in a clump of peasants' homes more than a mile from the ford.

Through the open door of the largest hovel, the monk could see three figures bent over a table in the gloomy interior; two were holding down a struggling man as the third cut into his side with a small knife. Carefully, the man with the knife probed the gaping hole. The patient convulsed each time the slender blade slid into his flesh; sobs of agony escaped from between his clenched teeth.

Unable to watch any more, the monk turned, knelt and began to pray over the corpses. The archer watched him, happy for the diversion from the monotony of guarding the dead.

"Here comes another," the sentinel sighed a moment later.

Thomas rose from his knees and turned to look. Two men approached, carrying the body of a young archer; carefully, they laid it at the end of the row, covering it with a blanket. Thomas realised it was the man he had seen writhing on the table moments before.

A short, middle-aged man emerged from the house. His thinning hair was grey, and he walked with a slight stoop. He was wiping his hands on the blood-soaked leather apron that reached to his knees.

"I am sorry that you could not give them some final comfort, brother," said the man, nodding at the row of corpses as he rubbed at the blackish blood streaking his fingers.

"I came as quickly as possible, but the directions were vague and it took some time to find this place," Thomas explained apologetically.

"Nay, brother, nay. I did not mean to reproach you."

The little man dropped the hem of the apron and laid a hand on Thomas's arm. His grip was firm and reassuring.

"I am William Bradwardyn, a surgeon, and you are most welcome." The man's eyes sparkled with warmth and kindness.

"Your pardon, Master Bradwardyn. I am Brother Thomas Elmham. Are there any who require the services of a priest?"

Bradwardyn shook his head. "Thankfully, no, although some of the wounded will doubtless welcome any kind words you may have to spare. Come. You are weary from your journey. Take some wine."

He turned back to the house without waiting for an answer. Following the surgeon through the low doorway, Thomas felt his knees buckle as he saw that the tabletop was covered with puddles of blood; scraps of flesh and bone floated on the crimson pools. The stench of blood, excrement and sweat buffeted his nostrils, making him gag.

Before Thomas knew what was happening, Bradwardyn spun him about, and led him outside. The surgeon guided the monk to a low wooden bench set against the hovel wall.

"That was thoughtless of me," he apologised. "I am so used to such things that I forget the effect they may have on even the hardiest spirits."

Thomas gulped gratefully at the cold air, fighting to keep down the sour vomit at the back of his mouth.

"Wine," Bradwardyn called to an attendant. A moment later a clay beaker was in Thomas's shaky hand.

"It is one of nature's best cures." The surgeon smiled as he took a second cup from the servant.

"Forgive me," Thomas said.

"Nay, brother. There is no need for apologies. Your reaction was quite natural," said the surgeon.

Bradwardyn sat next to Thomas and sighed as he leaned against the hovel wall, closing his eyes.

"What were you doing to that poor fellow?" Thomas asked.

"It was a procedure to stop bleeding, but the flow was too heavy. I failed and the poor devil died." The surgeon sighed. He turned and studied Thomas for a moment. "You are interested in the healing arts, brother?"

"Truly, Master Bradwardyn. I would be most grateful if you could tell me something of your profession."

Bradwardyn smiled. "My young friend, I could talk for a month, but we both have other demands on our time. Still, perhaps we may linger for a moment or two."

"I have heard the king did engage you, Master Bradwardyn?" Thomas asked.

"Indeed. The king spares no expense to provide medical care for the army. He hired both myself and my colleague Thomas Morstede. I have nine surgeons under me, and Morstede has twelve. We also have apothecaries, dressers of wounds and the like. It is widely said that the English army has better medical services than any other in Christendom."

Bradwardyn took another sip of wine.

"War is a ghastly business, my young friend," he continued, "but it cannot be denied that it has aided the art of healing greatly."

Seeing Thomas's quizzical expression, the surgeon explained.

"There has been great progress in healing many kinds of wounds. Arrows, for example. The chance of a cure depends largely on where a man is struck. If an arrow hits a fellow in the heart, then the poor wretch will almost certainly die. Likewise with deep wounds to the skull. And men spitted in the stomach rarely live, although we do not really understand why. Some say the juices of the gut or the bowels cause a rot in the flesh. With other parts of the body, however, there is often a good chance of saving a man's life, even if an arrow pierces him deeply. Some surgeons say the deeper the wound the better, because the best cure is to push the arrowhead straight out the other side. Pulling it back to the entry point, on the other hand, risks tearing a man's insides to pieces. But wounds are not just a question of life or death." The surgeon paused thoughtfully.

"What do you mean?" Thomas asked.

"For every fellow who is killed in battle there are two or three others who are maimed for life. Men may be blinded, left armless or legless, crippled with broken spines, castrated like a steer or suffer a hundred other misfortunes. Do you know, brother, I have always found that men are more afraid of losing their manhood than their eyes. It's a curious thing."

Bradwardyn saw Thomas was blushing, and smiled. The surgeon began to stand up.

"May I ask you one more question?" said the monk.

Bradwardyn leaned back against the wall. "I talk too much. You should not tempt me, brother.'"

"You have said the army is better equipped with medical services than any other. Why do you think this is so?"

"Perhaps we shall have greater need than any other army." Bradwardyn chuckled. "Nay, brother. Mind me not," he added. "The answer is simple: the king cares for the army in a way that few masters care for their followers. Some say that it is because he is a good soldier or a good king. I think it is all of those and something more."

"What is that?"

"The king himself has had great need of the surgeon's art." Bradwardyn smiled at the monk's puzzlement. "You did not know that our king was wounded in the battle at Shrewsbury?"

Thomas shook his head.

"Perhaps you are too young," Bradwardyn allowed. "It was at the start of his father's reign. Rebel barons under the duke of Northumberland allied with the Welsh to take the throne."

"Ah, yes. Of this I know," Thomas said. "It was a grievous fight."

"Grievous and bloody, brother. The two armies did great slaughter against each other. I have heard it said that of the nine thousand men on the field that day, no fewer than two thousand were slain, with many more wounded. Many of the dead were struck down by arrows."

Bradwardyn pondered for a moment before continuing.

"One of those who was hit was our king. He was then prince of Wales. His father had given him command of the left wing of the royal army. An arrow struck Henry in the face, piercing his cheek. Another inch higher and it would have been fatal, and you and I would not be sitting here now," the surgeon added.

Thomas nodded agreement. "My abbot says that the fate of nations is often decided by the most trivial actions or events."

"Your abbot is a wise man, brother. Fortunately, the king survived. It was not an easy recovery. The arrowhead was embedded in his face. It took all of the skill of one of my colleagues to remove it," Bradwardyn explained.

"How was it done?" the monk asked.

"The steel barb was lodged deep in the king's cheekbone. It took many days of probing and widening the wound until the arrowhead could be drawn out."

"It must have been a great ordeal."

"For Henry and the surgeon. Who wants to be blamed for the death of a future king?" Bradwardyn said. "They say that the king bore the agony without a word. Well, enough of that." The surgeon rose to his feet. "There are few pleasures in life as great as a willing and intelligent listener, but we both have work to do. I hope we may meet again, brother, when there will be time to talk."

"I hope so, Master Bradwardyn." Thomas grasped the man's proffered hand.

—— **20 OCTOBER** ——

Athies

The French heralds rode into the English camp at midday: three men resplendent in stiff white surcoats lined with gold fleurs-de-lys. Each herald held a staff of office in his right hand. Heralds were part of an international brotherhood guarded by the laws of chivalry, free to ride through enemy lines to convey messages or parley without fear of harm.

Three English heralds rode out to meet the French envoys at the first English guard post. Gravely, the men greeted each other; each one named himself and his office.

Henry was waiting in front of his tent in the centre of the camp. He was bareheaded, and dressed in his customary plain grey wool tunic and leather leggings. A sword hung at his side; his right hand in a stout leather gauntlet rested lightly on the hilt. Arrayed behind the king were his great nobles.

"Greetings," the king said simply when the English heralds had introduced their French counterparts.

"Henry of England!" began Montjoie, the chief French herald, a willowy man in his early fifties. "We bring a message from the king of all the French."

His two companions stood silent behind Montjoie. The English listened without a word.

"Know this, Henry of England" the herald continued in a voice that was as stern as his features. "A great army lies before you. One that you cannot hope to escape. You are commanded to yield and beg for mercy or be utterly destroyed."

"Who leads this army, good herald?" the king asked in his antiquated French.

"The dukes of Orleans and Bourbon, along with the Constable Albret and Marshal Boucicaut," the herald answered.

With a contemptuous glance at the ragged knights and archers looking on, the Frenchman continued, "We have seen your army, if such a rabble even deserves the term. You are greatly outnumbered. Your men are sweepings from the gutter. They are fit only for tending pigs. If you will submit to avoid needless slaughter, we will take your plea for mercy to the lords of France."

Some of the English lords muttered angrily at the herald's words. Henry raised the hand from his sword for silence.

"We yield to no man," he said calmly.

"Then you accept the challenge to battle?" the herald demanded.

"Tell your masters that we march to the sea. It will not be difficult to find us if they wish."

—— **21 OCTOBER** ——

Péronne

The French heralds had revealed the day before that Calais was still a hundred miles away, much further than the English had calculated after crossing the Somme. It was like a blow from an oak cudgel to the weary and hungry English troops. Hopes of reaching the sea and safely began to slip away during the night as the army huddled in the wet and windy fields. Captains and sergeants had to use their fists to rouse some of the soldiers at dawn, and force them to set out on the muddy track to the north-west.

Henry instructed the army to advance in battle order. Lords and knights rode in full armour. Every man nervously watched for signs of ambush. Icy rain lashed the army as it marched, half blinding the men, and drenching their ragged, stinking clothing.

"Eight poxy days. That's all it would take to reach Calais, they said. It's been almost twice that now," complained an archer in one of the contingents. "They drive us to the slaughter like old sheep."

Encouraged by murmurs from the men around him, the archer suddenly tossed away the wooden stake he had been carrying on his shoulder. "I won't carry it another inch. I'm not an ass to be whipped until I die," the man growled.

The rest of the band stopped. The archers warily eyed the stake lying by the verge: if one more man abandoned his wooden burden all of them would follow.

"Stop your whining, you whoreson, and pick up that stake," barked their captain. "Unless you'd rather be left here trussed up like a goose to give some French peasants a little carving practice."

The captain thrust his glaring face within an inch of the archer, his clenched fists half raised. With a curse, the man bent and picked up the stake. His companions shuffled on.

Such outbursts could be put down, but not even the king could do anything about the army's hollow bellies. There had been no bread for days, and the food wagons were all but empty. Hunger chiselled the soldiers' faces into living skulls; gleaming white boils glistened on their grimy necks. Men rummaged for nuts and berries on roadside bushes already stripped bare. In the abandoned villages they found only rotting fruit that had fallen from the trees weeks before. The hungriest tried to force down the putrid, worm-infested apples only to vomit or suffer agonising stomach cramps.

Hundreds fell sick as the flux which had ravaged the army at Harfleur reappeared in the ranks. Men dashed from the column to squat in the ditches to empty their bowels; others discarded their leggings, and whatever was left of their pride, letting the yellow slime trickle down their bare legs as they marched.

The army's physicians could do nothing. Men delirious with fever were half carried and half pulled by friends only slightly less ill. A handful of men deserted, slinking away, singly or in pairs, only to be hunted down and butchered by French peasants who emerged from their hiding places once the army had gone.

Five Miles beyond Péronne, Mid-Afternoon

Three horsemen were spotted as the English army emerged from a valley. Grassland and open fields stretched into the distance.

"Our scouts return," said Sir John Cornwall as he and Sir Gilbert Umfraville rode at the head of the vanguard. "What grim tale do they bring?"

The scouts' faces showed no emotion as the knights greeted them.

"What news, Hodge?" Cornwall asked their leader.

The scout gestured at the fields ahead. "See for yourself, Sir John."

He led the knights back across the fields. After a mile or so the grass gave way to crushed vegetation and torn earth covered with the prints of thousands of men and horses. It was clear that a vast army had passed that way a few hours earlier.

"How many, Hodge?" Cornwall asked.

The scout shrugged.

"How many devils are there in Hell?" came the reply.

Men gasped or cursed when they saw the tracks as the English army marched over them. Some of the soldiers looked up at the sky and loudly beseeched God to save them.

Only Henry seemed unperturbed. He did not smile or try to cheer the men as he rode up and down the column the rest of the day, telling the troops to straighten the lines or move more quickly. Wordlessly, men bowed their heads and went on.

— **23 OCTOBER** —

Doullens, 10:34 p.m.

"Halt!" The challenge was barely audible over the driving rain. The little pack of horsemen pulled up.

"Are you English?" came a challenge.

"I am English and England itself," the leading horseman called over the downpour.

The reply brought momentary confusion among the armed men blocking the rutted track. Their leader stepped forwards to peer through the darkness at the speaker.

"By your tongue you're English, whatever you may call yourself," he said doubtfully.

By now the soldier, a man well past thirty, had advanced far enough to recognise the king. Rain was streaming off Henry's helmet, cascading over his armoured shoulders and down his steel-clad chest.

"Pardon, sire. We was just doing our duty," the soldier humbly said.

"And you do it well, good fellow. What is your name?"

"Thomas Dawner, sire," the man answered. "We were set to guard the road."

"You have our thanks for your vigilance, Master Dawner."

At that moment the clatter of hooves drew their attention. A second group of horsemen emerged out of the night.

"Sire, are you well?" the man at their head called anxiously.

"You find us in the company of these good fellows, Sir Thomas," Henry answered. "How could we not be well?"

Sir Thomas Erpingham sceptically regarded the men blocking the road. Their faces were black with grime and stubble, and even the poorest beggar would have rejected the rags they wore.

"Is your captain and the rest of the company up ahead?" the king asked Dawner.

"Nay, sire." The man shook his head. "Ain't no one up that road except the French."

"What?" gasped one of the king's knights. "You mean you are alone?"

"Aye." Dawner showed his contempt at the question. "Nothing between us and the foe except the wind, rain and mud."

"Sire, the camp is some three miles back down the road with the main body of the army," Erpingham said. "Let us lead you there."

Henry motioned the knight to come closer so the others could not hear. "I am at the head of the army with the French just ahead. I will not do anything that might be seen as retreating or falling back," he said.

Before Erpingham could protest, the king said in a loud voice, "Master Dawner, might we share your watch this night?"

A fresh squall buffeted the knot of riders and footmen. Dawner wiped the heavy droplets from his eyes.

"Gladly, although we have no food or drink. Indeed, we have nothing to offer any man, let alone a king."

"No matter," Henry replied.

All through what was left of the night, the king of England and his knights stood guard in the rain with Dawner's little band.

—— **24 OCTOBER** ——

Blangy

The French came without warning. One moment the road was empty, and then the English suddenly saw a sea of armoured men advancing towards them. The soldiers gazed in horror and disbelief at the packed ranks of enemy horse and foot; those with experience in such things estimated the enemy must number at least thirty thousand men.

Henry deployed his little force for battle. There were only sufficient men to form a single line. Stakes were driven hurriedly into the earth in front of the archers. Boys and servants ran from the wagons with bundles of arrows as the priests beseeched Heaven to show mercy on the English cause.

Silently, the two armies eyed each other across the bare fields. The French soldiers could see how weak the English were; they grinned and slapped each other on the back, exulting at how easy their victory would be. The French commanders decided after an hour that it was too late in the day to attack. Waiting would only wear down the demoralised English further, they reasoned, and French reinforcements were arriving every hour.

It was late afternoon, when the French broke ranks. Some moved slowly, shouting final insults at the silent English, while others hurried off to claim whatever shelter could be found in the nearby villages.

Henry kept his men in position until well after the last of the enemy had vanished. Only the muttered prayers of some of the English soldiers broke the silence hanging over the darkening fields.

PART III

EVE OF BATTLE

—— 25 OCTOBER ——

King Henry's Quarters, Maisoncelle, 00:16 a.m.

Henry studied the sheets of parchment covering the crude wooden table. A solitary candle cast feeble shadows on the dingy clay walls of the one-room hovel; the peasant who lived there had fled with his family an hour before the English army occupied the hamlet. Filthy straw covering the earthen floor rustled each time the king moved. He was alone except for a clerk perched on a stool.

In a quiet, steady voice, Henry dictated orders for the coming battle. It was past midnight, but he showed no sign of weariness.

Sir John Cornwall pushed aside the grimy strip of sacking that served as the hovel's door, and entered, with Sir Gilbert Umfraville a step behind. Henry greeted the two men with a nod. Cornwall took in the room: the flea-ridden hole was barely fit to be an animal pen, and yet it was the best housing in the settlement.

Henry finished the dictation a minute later and dismissed the clerk with a wave of his hand before addressing the two knights.

"Good sirs. What news do you bring?"

"Sentries and watch fires are set around the camp perimeter, sire. The army has bedded down as best it can," Cornwall replied.

"How bad is it?" Henry asked.

"Bad enough. Most of the men are lying in the open fields. The lucky ones are sheltering in ditches. The rain keeps falling, and there is no food."

Henry looked at Umfraville.

"A dozen men have been sent to spy out the French lines, as you instructed," the younger knight said. "They will also try to scout the land where we can expect to fight."

"How far is the French camp?" Henry asked.

"Their main body is some two miles from here."

"Good." The king approved. "Summon the council to meet in one hour, when we will discuss the plans for the battle. Leave us now."

Cornwall and Umfraville bowed and silently left. Outside, the rain showed no sign of easing. Thick mud squelched beneath their feet as the knights walked.

The blazing bonfires of the French encampment illuminated the horizon. The din of thousands of men and animals echoed across the fields from the enemy lines as if they were just a few hundred feet away. A handful of feeble fires marked the English positions; the only movement was of sentries keeping watch. A passing traveller would not have guessed that an army lay huddled in the darkness.

"Well?" Umfraville enquired.

Cornwall looked at him.

"What will the day bring?" the young knight asked.

"Only God in his Heaven knows that, Gilbert," Cornwall's tone was bleak. "I only know that France is the greatest power in Christendom. Her knights are second to none in bravery and skill of arms. And we are outnumbered by at least six to one. They scent victory, and they lust for revenge – revenge for the shame of seeing their lands and homes violated, revenge for every defeat we have ever inflicted on them."

Umfraville nodded. "Most of our men expect to die."

"They may well be right. But first they will fight – fight like demons. If the French want us dead they will have to pay a heavy price in their own blood." Cornwall studied his companion for a moment before continuing, "Much will be decided in the coming hours: the fate of two armies, two nations and two crowns. It will all be played out on this miserable patch of mud."

French Camp, Agincourt, 00:45 a.m.

The French camp resembled a huge city on the busiest festival day of the year. Hundreds of roaring fires lit the long lines of tents and marquees. Thousands of jovial, laughing men thronged the bustling makeshift streets in between.

All of the great wealth of France was on display. Nobles and knights sported silk and satin robes with furs to ward off the autumn chill while even the humblest soldiers were clad in stout wool and linen suits. Every man was well armed, and richly decorated armour arrayed on wooden manikins stood outside each tent.

Slabs of beef, chickens and sausages sizzled on spits over the fires; men drank their fill from wooden barrels of wine open for all to dip their cups. Cheers erupted each time another band of reinforcements cantered into the encampment.

Few of the lords and soldiers had any thought of sleeping even if it might have been possible amid the clamour; none of them ever expected to see such a night again, and none of them wanted to miss a single moment.

Knights and soldiers wandered up and down the tented streets, greeting friends and companions. Young men laughed and joked as they practised with swords and lances; older men called out advice and made good-natured jests whenever one of the callow combatants misjudged a stroke or suffered a blow. All the talk was of the coming victory: no one thought of dying; only the English would perish.

"Why are we waiting to kill the English swine?" drunkenly roared a knight. "We should go and finish the bastards off now!"

"You'd get lost in the dark," one of the other men sitting around the fire laughed. Each man held a wine cup that had been filled and drained several times in the past hour.

"Are you saying I'm drunk, you guttersnipe?" the knight spluttered as he lurched to his feet. "Where's my sword?"

He turned to look for the weapon, and tripped over the stool he had been squatting on. His companions roared with laughter.

"Come, my friend. The English will still be there in the morning. Let us enjoy the evening," the other man soothed.

"Hey? Oh well, perhaps you're right." The knight sank back on the stool.

"Better to wait for dawn," growled a third man. "We want to see the look on their faces when we cut their throats."

King Henry's Quarters, Maisoncelle, 1:30 a.m.

"The French camp lies between the village of Agincourt and the smaller settlement of Tramecourt," the scout explained.

He sketched out the battlefield in thick black lines on the tabletop with a piece of charcoal as he spoke.

"Between us and the French lies a stretch of open fields some two miles long and about a mile wide with forest on either side. The fields are newly ploughed with deep furrows full of rainwater and mud. It won't be easy to cross, especially for mounted men."

"So the French are not likely to fight on horse?" Henry enquired.

"Aye, sire," the scout said. "As best as we can judge."

Henry studied the crude map. He was not sure the English army had enough men to hold its end of what resembled a long jousting field. At least the forests running along the sides of the fields should keep them from being outflanked.

"Anything else?" he asked the scout.

The man, who had given his report crisply and confidently, looked unsure for the first time.

"You have done valiant work. We value anything you say," the king reassured him.

"Well, it's just that I was able to cross the French lines and walk through part of their camp. There were so many that one more was not noticed," the scout said.

"A brave feat. What did you discover?"

"I have never seen men so eager for a fight. It was as if they had already won the battle and were celebrating victory."

Bleak silence followed the man's words.

"Our thanks." The king motioned the scout to leave.

"May the Almighty protect you, sire." The man bowed on one knee before leaving.

Henry looked at the members of the council standing around the table.

"There can be advantages in being so few. It won't take long to deploy the army," he quipped. A few of the lords smiled. "This is how we will fight –" Henry gestured at the map – "We have sufficient men to form a single line. The nobles and men-at-arms numbering some nine hundred and sixty swords will be in the middle. They will fight on foot in three bodies. I shall command the centre one, the duke of York the right and Lord Camoys the left. Our archers, numbering some five thousand, will be divided equally into two groups on the flanks."

Henry had chosen wisely. York was the most senior of the nobles and Camoys the eldest; both were experienced leaders –

factors all of the proud and jealous lords could stomach even if their pride was ruffled at not being given a command.

"Are there any other matters?" the king asked. After a pause, he continued, "The camp will stay silent for the rest of the night so the army may spend the time in quiet prayer. Any man who breaks the peace will be punished. A noble shall pay a fine of a horse, a commoner shall lose his right ear."

Henry's words visibly shocked several of the lords.

"It is a harsh command, sire," the young earl of Suffolk said.

"It will allow the army to make its peace with God. Men should spend what might be their last night on earth in prayer. That way they will be able to face whatever may come with clear consciences," the king replied.

French Camp, Agincourt, 1:30 a.m.

For two hours the French war council had argued over plans for the coming day. The air in the tent reeked of sweat, wine and acrimony. The younger lords clamoured to attack, insisting that a single charge would crush the English under an avalanche of French steel and valour. They jeered whenever the older man at the head of the table urged caution.

Boucicaut, marshal of the French army, was a legendary warrior who embodied the chivalric virtues of bravery, fidelity and modesty. Only his appearance fell short of the knightly ideal: he was squat and muscular with the battered face of a tavern brawler. The marshal had fought his first battle thirty years previously, whereas many of the men at the table had never shed blood. But for all his great achievements, Boucicaut was of humble origins, and the princes and dukes on the council refused to defer to him.

"I have seen the destruction the English archers inflict," the marshal insisted for the third time. "No amount of breeding or courage can save a man from an arrow that can strike him down from three hundred yards."

Charles, the duke of Orleans, ostentatiously yawned as Boucicaut spoke. Several of the other lords smirked at the insult. Although just twenty, Charles was the pre-eminent noble in the army because his uncle and namesake was king. He was brave and tempestuous, a noted jouster and a celebrated writer of love poetry; he was also inexperienced, rash and convinced he should command the army in the absence of the king and the crown prince.

"Marshal, we are all in awe of your legendary feats." There were titters at Orleans' insulting drawl. "And your tales of ancient history are doubtless fascinating."

Charles d'Albret, the constable of France, sitting besides Boucicaut, stiffened with anger.

"Hear the puppy out," Boucicaut muttered.

"We have the largest army that France has fielded in many years – thirty thousand to their mere six thousand," Orleans went on. "More importantly, our ranks are full of men of noble blood. You have seen the English rabble. They have but a handful of men-at-arms. The rest are peasants, low-born filth. The English archers you seem so fearful of will run as soon as we attack."

There were roars of agreement. Several of the council members hammered their fists on the table in applause, others laughed with pleasure. Orleans' vision of an easy and glorious victory enraptured them.

Boucicaut felt anger and despair pressing at his temples. He had witnessed such pig-headed posturing on the eve of other battles, and seen the corpses of those who had boasted of their own invincibility. The council had already sent home most of the army's crossbowmen; it said they were not needed, but the real reason was that Orleans and many of the nobles despised them for being commoners.

"Bravery alone cannot win a battle," Boucicaut protested.

The plea was met with scowls from the young nobles.

"So you would have us run away rather than fight?" challenged Orleans.

"Of course not." There was anger in the marshal's voice for the first time. "Can't you see that all the advantages are on our side. The English are trapped. Time, hunger and cold will force them to surrender. All we have to do is block their way and wait."

"Ha!" Orleans snorted. "Always wait, wait, wait. Waiting is for old women. I came here to kill this English upstart Henry."

"A battle is no certain thing," Boucicaut struggled to speak calmly. "Too much can go wrong, too much is unpredictable. Even the biggest and bravest armies may be defeated."

"So, you expect us to lose? Is that it?" Orleans' cheeks flushed with fury.

"I expect nothing. No soldier worth his salt does."

Furious protests drowned out the marshal. He stared at the ring of red, angry faces glaring at him from around the table. It was pointless to argue; the mood in the tent was close to the shedding of blood. At last he gave in, and a battle plan was sulkily agreed on.

The bulk of the army would be divided into three divisions. Two divisions, each with ten thousand nobles, knights and men-at-arms, would form the first and second lines and fight on foot. The third division, of three thousand mounted men, would be in the rear. Two separate contingents of mounted men on the flanks would charge at the start of the battle and sweep away the English archers. The first division would then advance to attack the English men-at-arms. The second division would follow and help complete the slaughter. At the same time a force under the lord of Agincourt would attack the English camp in the rear. Finally, the third division would ride down any surviving English who tried to run. The rest of the army would guard the French camp.

"To victory," the duke of Alençon bellowed as he raised a silver goblet in a pudgy fist. Red wine coursed down his plump cheeks, cascading off his chin as he tried to empty it in a single draught.

English Camp, Maisoncelle, 2:43 a.m.

Henry gazed at the blazing lights of the French encampment. Thousands of English soldiers huddled or slept unseen in the darkness around him. His order for the army to pass the night in quiet prayer had hardly been necessary. An exhausted silence cloaked the camp. Any men still awake were lost in thoughts of home and what might be their final hours. Even the horses, tethered in long lines, were silent, as if sensing what the morning would bring.

Henry paused by one of the watch fires. A group of archers sat or lay around it. Many of the men were asleep; one muttered incoherently as he dreamed.

"Sir." A tall archer stood at Henry's side. The king's face was hidden by the hood of his long black cloak.

"Do you require assistance?" asked the man.

"What is your name, good fellow?" Henry said.

"Nicholas Longford, sir." The archer did not ask the stranger's identity; his voice of command marked him for a noble.

"I require nothing," Henry said, "except a moment or two of your time."

"Not much of that," Longford gruffly replied. "Time, I mean."

"You fear the morrow?"

"What, the battle?" Longford asked.

Henry nodded.

"Any man who says he is not fearful is lying."

"Even the king?" Henry asked.

Longford was silent for a moment. "Not my place to talk of them that's my betters," he replied guardedly.

"It is an honest question. Fear not to answer it."

The archer stared doubtfully at the shrouded man then shrugged. "Aye. Any man with a heart knows fear at a time like this, and our king has a great heart."

"A good answer." Henry smiled. "You are content to follow him into the battle?"

"No man wants to die, but I am a soldier. I will follow Harry because it is my duty, and he is a worthy king." There was neither flattery nor doubt in his reply.

"And what of your men? Do they think the same?"

"Most of them expect to have their brains dashed out by a French axe or a sword rammed through their guts. But they will fight for all of that."

"The French greatly outnumber our army," Henry persisted.

"They have hunted us across this accursed country as if we were dogs. The men are tired of running. Let them come, no matter how many."

Silence followed Longford's declaration. Henry reached out and clasped the man's arm. Startled, Longford pulled back.

"I thank you for your words, and pray you will survive the battle," the king said.

"Who were that poxy bladder?" one of the men by the fire muttered as Henry's silhouette disappeared in the darkness.

"I don't know, but there were something familiar about him." Longford shrugged.

French Camp, Agincourt, 3:02 a.m.

Boucicaut and d'Albret gratefully breathed in the cool night air. They had left the tent as soon as the battle plan was completed.

"Perhaps Orleans is right. Age has made me too cautious." There was a sour note of doubt in Boucicaut's voice.

"Nonsense. You speak the truth. What man is ever thanked for that," the constable replied.

"Christ died for speaking the truth," the marshal said. Boucicaut was deeply religious; he habitually dressed in plain black in honour of the saviour's martyrdom.

"Always the priest, eh, Boucicaut?" d'Albret gently joked.

The marshal smiled, shrugging off his despondency.

"What think you of the plan?" the constable changed the subject.

"Plans are apt to be the first thing to perish in a battle. If it is to have any chance of working, a plan requires discipline and cohesion."

The constable nodded. "And we have a mob rather than an army. A mob led by cocksure braggarts and quarrelling infants."

"What are they up to?" Boucicaut pointed to some knights and squires clustered around a small wooden cart. The laughing men were decorating its sides with red and blue ribbons.

"Have you not heard?" the constable replied. "The lord of Croy and seventeen other young gallants have taken a vow to strike the crown from the English king's head."

"And the cart?"

"It will be used to parade Henry through the streets of Paris dressed only in his shirt."

Boucicaut laughed. "That will be a great day for France."

English Camp, Maisoncelle, 3:14 a.m.

Sir John Cornwall found Thomas in the broken-down shed where the knight's retinue had set up quarters. Half of the thatched straw roof had fallen in; great cracks split two of the mud walls. It was opulent compared to the open ground where most of the troops were lying in the rain.

"Thomas," Cornwall greeted the monk. "I wanted to see you."

"How so, Sir John?"

"The coming day will not be an easy one, lad. You have an outsized curiosity which ordinarily does you credit, but I do not want you anywhere near the battlefield when the blood-letting begins. It will be no place for innocents."

Thomas nodded. He knew there was no point in arguing.

"You will do your part in the rear praying to the Almighty to aid us," the knight continued. "Something we shall need greatly."

"You doubt that we will win?"

"Who knows? The strangest things can happen. David slew Goliath."

"And will King Henry slay him again?"

Cornwall chuckled. "God's teeth, boy. Let us hope so."

"Tell me, Thomas," he continued, "who is this saint I heard the king's chaplain prattling about? Today is his name day. Christopher? Cuthbert?"

"Two saints," Thomas explained enthusiastically. "Crispin and Crispinian. They are the patron saints of shoemakers, saddlers and tanners."

"Leatherworkers?" the knight sounded doubtful.

"Oh, they were most holy men."

"Tell me their story. Briefly," Cornwall said.

"They lived in the time of ancient Rome here in France, and were martyred for their Christian faith. It is said the attempts of the executioners to kill them were confounded many times over. They were hurled into the river, but did not drown and the fire they were subjected to did not harm them."

"How did they die?

"The executioners cut their heads off."

Thomas fell silent. His story suddenly did not seem very cheering: if God's saints could die, he thought, what hope had mortal men outnumbered by a vast enemy?

"Well that's fine, then," Cornwall interrupted his thoughts.

"Sir John?" the puzzled monk asked.

"Your saints won't smile on the descendants of those who killed them. So they'll fight for us. Quite useful to have a few thunderbolts hurled about."

Thomas blushed when he realised he was smiling at the knight's blasphemous wit.

King Henry's Quarters, Maisoncelle, 3:30 a.m.

Henry found a visitor when he returned to his headquarters.

"De Gaucourt. I had not expected to find you here," the king said.

"Forgive me, sire. I would ask a favour," replied the French knight.

"A favour?" Irony tinged Henry's voice. "I may soon have nothing to give anyone if your countrymen have aught to do with it."

"Allow me to remain with the army, sire."

Henry looked surprised. All of the French prisoners had been released on condition that they return if the English won the battle. Most had gone off beaming or laughing, sure they would never have to keep their promises.

"Why do you wish such a thing? Will you fight for me?" Henry challenged.

De Gaucourt smiled. "I cannot do that, but I have marched with your army and made friends. I would not leave you now."

"You are an honourable man, de Gaucourt. Stay with my stewards in the rear."

De Gaucourt bowed in acknowledgement. He was turning to leave when Henry spoke.

"You know that I cannot guarantee your safety," the king said. "It may be dangerous to be a lone Frenchman in the midst of an English army fighting for its life. And if the day does not go well for us your own people may take exception if they find you in our lines."

"I understand," the knight replied.

THE BATTLE

25 OCTOBER

The English Camp, Maisoncelle, 5:08 a.m.

It was still an hour before dawn. Some of the English soldiers slept; many more lay awake or sat hunched under sodden blankets. Others sharpened axes and knives or oiled the leather straps of rusty armour. A lucky few breakfasted on handfuls of dry grain as hard as pebbles; the rest tried to ignore the ache of their empty bellies. The cloying stench of unwashed bodies, sodden clothing and excrement covered everything.

An archer knelt in the mud before Thomas. A hood hid the man's face; a battered cowhide jerkin hung loosely over his chest, which was hollowed out by hunger and marching. But the monk could feel a steely strength in the fingers clutching at his hand.

"Bless me, brother," the man mumbled in a thick burr. Three months ago such an accent would have baffled the monk. Now, he understood every dialect in the army as if he had spoken them all his life. The soldiers had become his family, he mused, these rough, violent men who knew nothing about learning or piety.

Thomas recited a blessing in Latin, and made the sign of the cross over the archer's bowed head. A dozen men had approached him in as many minutes to ask for absolution. Apprehension clouded the eyes of some, others seemed resigned or almost serene. None was dissatisfied or angry that Thomas could only spare him a few hurried words; each man nodded gratefully or mumbled thanks as he rose from his knees.

King Henry's Quarters, Maisoncelle, 5:10 a.m.

Henry knelt in full armour before the little makeshift altar. Three royal chaplains chanted the words of the mass, their rich baritones filling the hovel with a fleeting beauty. When the last words had faded away, the king reached for the helmet resting on the straw-covered floor beside him and stood; a gold crown encircled the burnished steel dome. Wordlessly, he ducked through the low doorway. A dozen mounted knights of the royal household waited in the pre-dawn darkness. Henry mounted effortlessly and rode into the gloom.

English Battle Line, 5:42 a.m.

A company of archers trudged past the king. Every soldier in the English army wore a red cross on his breast so that foe and friend would recognise him in the coming battle. The archers' emblems were crudely cut from cheap cloth and clumsily sewn on their leather and wool jackets. A few of the men possessed old iron helmets, the rest wore hoods or felt hats.

Henry watched from the side of the track as other contingents followed. The captains at the head of each band inclined their heads, but there was no other acknowledgement of the king's presence. He studied the passing men. How many, he wondered, would still be alive by sunset?

*   *   *

One by one, the contingents wheeled into their places in the slender English battle line. It was only then that the soldiers saw the French arrayed on the other side of the field. Many gasped in disbelief at the size of the enemy host. The French ranks seemed to stretch as far as they could see. Tens of thousands of armoured men stood in rows in the French centre. Contingents of mounted knights were forming up on each flank.

"God help us, captain," whispered John Hampton. "We are too few."

"Perhaps," drily responded Robert Alderton. "Still, they make a wondrous target. Even a half-blind useless fellow like you won't miss for once."

French Battle Line, 6:01 a.m.

The roar of thousands of happy voices and laughter boomed over the French lines. All the talk was of the coming victory, and how easy it would be. Men pointed at the little English force across the fields and joked about going to England to comfort the thousands of women who would be widows before the day was done. Servants with flagons of wine weaved among the lords and knights, keeping their masters' cups full; scullions from the kitchens proffered wooden boards heaped with steaming hunks of roasted meat and fresh bread.

Hundreds of flags fluttered over the sea of armoured men. Each banner was emblazoned with the crest of a great noble family; centuries of chivalry and tradition were etched in their intricate images and patterns. Blue, white and red silk streamers fluttered from the helmets of the knights, tokens from wives and sweethearts to give their loved ones victory, and bring them home safely.

Many of the nobles and knights vied with each other in boasting of how many of the accursed English they would personally send to their graves; none of the swine would ever see his wretched little island again. A young lord described how he would lead the English king through the streets of Paris on foot behind his horse.

"With a noose around his unwashed neck," he shrieked as his friends guffawed.

Old rivalries were put aside. Men whose houses and families had been enemies for decades embraced. Some swore to fight side by side in the battle. It brought tears to the eyes of hardened killers for whom slitting a man's throat was as mundane as cracking an egg at breakfast.

Only the officers tasked with making sure the army took up its positions were not joining in the carnival mood.

"Get into line, damn you," shouted a knight. With a curse, he lashed at a group of men-at-arms with the wooden baton that was his badge of office.

A grizzled nobleman saw what was happening. "Shit breath! How dare you strike my men," he bellowed. The nobleman's plump cheeks purpled with rage; white specks of saliva flew from his mouth.

"Stand back," warned the knight. "I am an officer of Marshal Boucicaut's household."

"That low-born knave," howled the nobleman. "If you serve that peasant you are a craven cur."

"How dare you?" The knight waved his baton at the nobleman; it was decorated with royal fleur-de-lis to denote his authority.

"Stick it up your arse," snarled the nobleman. "I am the count of Roucy."

"You are charged with taking your assigned place," the knight retorted. "You must obey."

"I take orders from no man," the count roared.

Roucy's bloodshot, malicious eyes dared the knight to attack. The count's men gripped their weapons. The knight hesitated;

starting a brawl in the French ranks did not seem the best way of carrying out his orders.

"Sir," he tried to reason. "We are here to fight the English, not each other."

"Ha," the noble sneered. "You are a gutless pansy who would rather fondle little boys than fight men."

For a moment, the knight, his face white with fury, tensed. Then he shook his head, turned and walked away. Mocking taunts followed him.

"Idiots," he fumed. "This is an army. Can't they comprehend there must be order and discipline."

His deputy nodded agreement. "It is happening everywhere. None of the nobles will defer to each other," the man said.

Each contingent in the French army had been assigned a place on the battlefield. Scores of princes and lords had ignored the orders, insisting it was their right to be in the front ranks as the place of greatest honour. Many nobles had forced their way to the head of the army with their retainers.

"The army is all leaders and no followers," fumed the knight, surveying the heaving chaos of jostling, arguing men. "Still, we will triumph." He motioned at the slender line of English troops in the distance. "All our high-born oafs have to do is walk over them."

English Battle Line, 6:01 a.m.

A thousand yards away, the English silently watched. The small band of men-at-arms stood in four rows in the centre of the English battle line with the archers deployed on either side. There had been no pushing or arguing for space or prominence as the army formed up: every man was in the front ranks, with wide gaps between each of them.

The lie of the ground appeared to give the English their only advantage. The newly ploughed fields sloped gently down from the English lines to the French: the enemy would have to advance uphill if they attacked.

"How many of the snail-eaters?" Umfraville asked Cornwall as they stood in the English front rank. The din of voices, drums and the tramp of armoured men rolled over the fields from the enemy lines.

"More than enough," came the reply.

"More than enough for what?"

"More than enough to stop your endless questions."

Umfraville eyed Cornwall.

"Something clouds your thoughts, Sir John?" he said after a moment.

"What?" Cornwall was momentarily taken aback by the question. "No. I was just wondering if the world has ever seen an army like ours," he said. "Most of our men are ploughboys, poachers and peasants. Lads as unkissed by breeding and the laws of chivalry as the pigs they tended as children in their fathers' hovels. If we survive, the poets and bards are going to have their work cut out turning this lot into gallants and heroes."

Swarms of archers pounded stakes into the earth in front of the English battle line. Some of the sweating men wielding wooden hammers were stripped to the waist despite the late October chill. As the stakes were lodged firmly in place, men with axes and adzes sharpened the tops; each jagged point was angled at the height of a horse's chest.

Once the stakes were erected, the archers tested their bows. Arrows were checked to ensure the steel heads were secure, and tail feathers given a final flourish. Clumps of arrows were thrust in the ground by each man's right foot, ready for use.

"Not so deep, you're not planting trees," a sergeant chided a young archer. "You don't want to waste time tugging them free when we fire."

"Aye, sergeant," the archer mumbled.

The sergeant saw the youth was deathly white. "Bear up, lad," he said softly.

Startled, the youth began to insist nothing was amiss, then looked appealingly at the sergeant.

"I fear I will die this day," he blurted.

"There's no shame in feeling fear. It afflicts all of us."

"You too?" the youth doubtfully asked.

"All of us, boy. Every man feels the fear pressing on his chest or gripping his guts. It will disappear as soon as the fight begins. There will be no time for thinking then – only for cutting down those French sons of whores before they do the same to us."

English Centre, 6:10 a.m.

Henry sat astride his horse in front of the English battle line. The king in his blue, red and gold surcoat adorned with golden leopards and lilies was a startling splash of colour amid the drab ranks. Five knights stood behind him with banners adorned with the emblems of the royal house. At their centre was the flag of England, the red cross of Saint George on a snow-white field.

Everything about the young king's attire and position had been calculated to ensure he stood out. It was unspoken proof to his filthy and haggard men that he would lead them to victory or die with them.

"Some say our king resembles the young Alexander the Great," said an admiring knight in Lord Camoys' contingent.

Camoys, who looked less than noble in rust-streaked armour intended to conceal his identity as a senior commander, sniffed.

"It is well known that Alexander was dead at the age of thirty-three."

"But he had conquered the world first," replied the knight, not caring if he offended his master.

"Good sir, what is the time?" Henry enquired of the chaplain standing by his horse. The cleric scanned the sun emerging above the nearby trees.

"It is almost prime, time for the first prayers of the day, sire."

"Good. People in England are awake. And while they cannot know what we face this day, they will doubtless pray for our safety and success. That will please God, and incline him to give us victory."

"Sir Thomas," Henry summoned the knight standing near by. Erpingham's armour was covered with a green surcoat decorated with black ravens. "It is time to speak to the men."

Henry nosed his mount forwards, advancing ten yards before wheeling to face the army.

"The king." The words rustled through the ranks until every eye was fixed on him.

Henry began to speak. He had shared his soldiers' fears, privations and dangers in a dozen campaigns; he knew what moved them, and he knew how to talk to them.

"Hear me. No one knows better than a soldier that war is a terrible thing. To die on the battlefield far from home and friends is a fate no man welcomes. And yet there are far worse things. Not to fight would be to forsake our honour and our manhood, and betray everything that we hold dear. We fight for what is right; we fight for England; we fight for God and his saints."

Henry looked in turn at the massed bowmen on the two flanks. "Archers! Remember the fate that awaits you if you fall into the hands of the enemy. The French lords have sworn to sever your fingers for daring to fight against them. And if they do not then butcher you like pigs, you will be cripples for the rest of your days."

Raising his right hand as if taking a solemn oath, Henry cried: "We shall all share the same fate this day. I promise that I will fight among you, and die among you, if Heaven is not with us. Fight for your honour and your king. Fight for your wives, children and aged parents at home. Fight for England."

A thunderous roar erupted from the ranks, swelling as it surged down the lines. "Henry! Henry!" thousands of voices roared.

French Battle Line, 6:12 a.m.

The cheers of the English army went almost unnoticed amid the clamour and laughter in the French ranks.

"Did you hear that?" a man-at-arms asked. He was staring across the muddy field, one shoulder leaning on a poleaxe lodged in the mud.

"What?" distractedly replied his companion, busy cracking nut shells.

"It's the English. They are cheering."

"Cheering?" The other man paused to peer at the English line. "What do those ugly toads have to cheer about?"

"Who knows?" answered his companion. "How can any sane man understand the English?"

Word of the baffling English behaviour was sent back to the French commanders. The approach of battle had not eased the tension of the night before. Boucicaut was arguing against ordering an immediate attack.

"You seem a little dyspeptic this morning, marshal," Orleans jeered. "Something you ate has disagreed with you? Or perhaps the prospect of the coming fight unsettles your stomach?"

Several of the younger lords snickered; the duke of Alençon guffawed.

Boucicaut glowered at his smirking tormentor.

"Surely, you do not take offence at my whimsy?" Orleans laughed.

Constable d'Albret angrily turned on Orleans. "Enough of this! Henry of England is not wasting time trading insults with his nobles."

Orleans' cheeks reddened with anger. Two of his courtiers protested.

The constable cut them off, "We must decide what to do."

"Yes," agreed Boucicaut. "What is your wish, your grace?"

Orleans was stunned. He had been demanding the right to command, but now that it seemed within his grasp he was unsure.

"What do you suggest, constable?" the duke hesitantly turned to d'Albret.

Boucicaut brusquely interjected, "We wait to see what the English do. Time is on our side, and we must give the ground a chance to dry out."

Orleans glared, but did not protest. Curtly, he nodded assent. One of his young followers leaned forwards, whispering something. Orleans beamed. "Unfurl the Oriflamme!" he demanded. "Show the English they can expect no mercy!"

It was clear from their expressions that neither Boucicaut or d'Albret liked the idea. The Oriflamme was a banner raised in extreme cases to show that no prisoners would be taken. The marshal knew that raising it was likely to make the English fight harder. Rebuffing Orleans, on the other hand, would cause more dissension among the French leaders. He reluctantly nodded assent.

Orleans yelped triumphantly as his sycophants clamoured: "The Oriflamme! Raise the Oriflamme! Death to the English!"

Guillaume de Martel, keeper of the Oriflamme, was summoned. The old lord, who was in his early sixties, unfurled the plain blood-red banner with a confident sweep of his hands. It snapped smartly in the breeze as thousands of awed men stared at the legendary symbol.

"That silenced them," d'Albret said to Boucicaut.

"Will it do the same to the English?" the marshal asked sourly.

English Battle Line, 6:15 a.m.

After the cheers following Henry's speech, priests moved swiftly along the English line. Every soldier knelt on the muddy ground, heads bared and bowed, hands clasped in prayer. The priests recited blessings and made the sign of the cross over the silent ranks.

"Defend our cause for it is just, O Lord. Destroy the ungodly and wicked French," implored one cleric, stretching his arms to the heavens. "Do not forsake us, we beseech thee."

The priests completed the blessings and began walking to the rear. Some went quickly. Others trailed behind, reluctant to leave.

"Do not linger, good brother," an archer told Thomas.

"I am afraid, and yet it seems shameful not to stay," the monk stammered.

"No need of you dying," the archer gently smiled. "There'll be more than enough who meet their end today."

Henry stood in the centre of the front rank after a squire led away his horse. The faces of the soldiers behind him were mostly blank; each man was alone with his own thoughts. And so they silently stood, waiting for the enemy to roll down on them in a great wave of steel and razor-sharp death.

English Lines, 10:23 a.m.

For four hours the English army had waited. The ranks were silent except for the clink of armour or a banner flapping in a gust of wind. A few ragged clouds raced across the slate-grey sky.

Henry stood alone in front of the army. He checked the ascent of the pale sun for the third time in as many minutes; the morning was more than half over. His gaze turned back to the French army. Still there was no sign of movement.

Strategy dictated that the outnumbered English must wait for the French to attack. For the English to move first would be considered utter madness. Henry weighed the situation as he studied the enemy lines: time was on the side of the French. His men were tired and famished, their morale was crumbling and there was no escape. At that moment he saw what had to be done.

French Lines, 10:24 a.m.

The mood in the French ranks was cheerful and relaxed. Men stood with their friends, joking and slapping backs. There was much talk of the poor fighting abilities of the English. Large sums were bet on how long it would take to finish the enemy off or if they would just drop their weapons and run. As the time went by, some lords sent for refreshments to ease the wait.

"Don't worry, Gaston," a baron laughingly bellowed at a plump red-faced page trying to balance a wooden tray loaded with meat and a brimming pitcher of wine as he shouldered his way through the ranks. "Tonight, the English king will wait on us at the victory feast. And you can sit on your fat arse," he roared as his retinue laughed.

English Lines, 10:25 a.m.

Henry sent two knights scurrying in either direction along the English battle line to summon his commanders. Moments later, he was joined by York, Camoys and the others.

"We cannot remain here all day," the king began. "Each hour that goes by weakens us. The men are tired, hungry and uncertain. I fear they will lose all hope if we simply wait for the French."

He saw a mix of reluctant agreement on their faces.

"We must fight. It is our only chance," he continued. "We will advance to bring our archers in range of the enemy."

The men facing him looked stunned. It was against all the lessons of war and the dictates of common sense for a small force to abandon a secure position and attack a far larger opponent. The army would be completely exposed as it slogged across the muddy ground. A French cavalry charge could catch them strung out and defenceless.

"How far must we advance for the archers to be in range of the enemy?" Henry asked Cornwall.

The knight studied the distant French lines, and the intervening ground.

"A good half-mile, at least. It will take ten minutes or more to cover the distance," he said.

The advance would be hard for men in full armour, and it would be hardest for those who were no longer young, a description that fitted most of the men around the king.

Henry interrupted their gloomy musings. "Instruct the captains to have the archers pull up their stakes. The army will advance on my command."

English Lines, 10:28 a.m.

The army's shock at the king's decision lasted only a moment. Men stared at each other in disbelief: some looked as if they had just heard their own death sentences. And then the bark of the captains and the habit of discipline took over. Thousands of archers wrested the wooden stakes out of the mud, grunting and cursing with the effort. Arrows were carefully slid back into leather quivers. The armoured men-at-arms, stiff from standing for hours, stretched and rolled their muscles as much as their iron and steel shells would allow. None of them wanted to be slow or stumble when the order to advance came, in case it looked as if they were reluctant or afraid.

Sir Thomas Erpingham went up and down the lines. With waves of his baton, he straightened the formations, ensuring there were no gaps. Once he was satisfied, the knight strode out in front of the army, turned and hurled the rod into the air.

"Now strike!" he cried.

In the hush that followed, Henry strode forwards alone until he was a good twenty yards in front of the army. There he knelt facing the enemy, and bowed his head, clasped hands resting on the hilt of his sword standing before him like a cross. Wordlessly, the army sank to its knees and prayed. As they finished, many of the men reached down, took a pinch of earth, and put it in their mouths. This was to fulfil the words of the burial service – "earth to earth, ashes to ashes, dust to dust" – in case the army was destroyed, and their bodies left unburied to rot in the fields.

English Lines, 10:30 a.m.

Henry rose from his knees. Without a single command, the army stood. The young king turned and faced the ranks. He gazed at the men, at the haggard faces streaked with dirt, exhaustion and fear. A smile momentarily softened his usually stern mouth.

"In the name of Saint George, raise the banners," the king cried in a voice the entire army could hear. A score of knights and squires stepped from the front rank, each man clasping a flag.

With a last look, Henry said simply: "Fellows, let us go."

And with that he turned and walked, alone and unguarded, towards the French lines. Thousands of men caught their breath; others felt their hearts pound or legs tremble. And then with a single roar, the army followed him.

French First Division, 10:32 a.m.

The English advance went unnoticed in the French ranks for a minute or two. Many of the soldiers had started to think nothing would happen that day. Some of the men grumbled at not being allowed to advance and finish off the English. Many more, tired by the waiting, and the heaviness of their armour, wanted to go back to their tents.

Scouts positioned ahead of the front line were the first to spot the approaching English banners, and then the thin line of men marching under them.

Gawking, curious soldiers peered and jostled to see what was happening after the first shouted warnings. Surprise, shock and disbelief shot through the French ranks as news of the enemy's outlandish behaviour spread back through the ranks. It soon turned to scorn and ridicule.

"The poor fools can't wait to die," a watching knight marvelled.

English Advance, 10:33 a.m.

The English advanced slowly, to keep their ranks straight and prevent gaps opening up. Every man slipped and stumbled as they trudged through the mud that soon coated their legs to the knees. It was hardest going for the men in armour, but the archers also laboured under the weight of the wooden stakes each of them carried. Stronger men aided weaker and elderly companions with steadying hands, grunting words of encouragement.

Heads and shoulders bowed, young and old, weak and strong, the English soldiers struggled through the muck, glancing up every two or three steps at the enemy. Every one of them knew that a French cavalry charge would cut them to pieces if they were caught in the open.

French Left Flank, 10:35 a.m.

"Mount!" screamed Clignet de Brabant, commander of the cavalry on the left flank of the French army. "Mount, damn you!"

De Brabant hammered an iron-gloved fist on his armoured hip in frustration as confused men and horses milled around him. Most of the six hundred riders he commanded, bored by hours of waiting and inactivity, had wandered off to rest or exercise their mounts in the rear. The same thing had happened in other contingents. Pandemonium engulfed the French army, with thousands of men pushing and shoving to get back to their places in the battle line as word of the English advance spread.

"Prepare to attack!" de Brabant thundered at the handful of his men who were still with him.

"We are too few," protested a knight, trying to control his nervous steed. "We need more men."

De Brabant hesitated. To attack with the few riders he had would be folly. He looked again at the advancing English.

"Find the others!" he roared at the knight. "Hurry!"

English Advance, 10:38 a.m.

Hearts pounding, sweat running down their faces and backs, the English halted some three hundred yards from the French. Frantically, the archers drove the stakes into the soft ground for a second time that morning. Men swarmed about the poles, pounding them with hammers, and then sharpening the tops.

The bowmen kept glancing over their shoulders at the enemy lines as they laboured, fearing attack at any moment. Some men rushed the work and did not ram the stakes deep enough or angled them too low. Angry captains and sergeants drove them back with curses and punches to mend their mistakes.

Every man worked frenziedly, every second expecting the warning cry that the enemy were coming. But the seconds turned to minutes, and the French did not move. Soon a thick fence of stakes carpeted the ground in front of the new English line. Only a gap in the centre where the English men-at-arms stood was left open.

English Lines, 10:40 a.m.

An archer raised his right hand, and baring his teeth in a wolfish grin, mocked the watching French with two fingers raised in a V-shape. Others saw the gesture and realised he was daring the enemy to sever his bow fingers. With bellows of defiance and laughter, they jerked their own fingers at the foe.

"Come and choke on some English steel, you milk-livered foot-lickers," one man roared.

English Left Flank, 10:40 a.m.

Captain John Selby studied his men as they jeered at the enemy. His company was the anchor at the far end of the English left flank. Despite the laughter, many of the faces of the archers were pale and uneasy. Selby beckoned to his sergeants. "To me," he called. He lowered his voice so only they could hear his words. "You must watch the men closely. The younger lads are as raw as turnips, and some of the older men should have hung up their bows long ago. It only takes one or two to take to his heels, and the line will break. If that happens the French will cut us down like newborn lambs."

Selby paused.

"You will stop any man who runs. Even if that means sticking a blade in their bellies. The only way we walk off this field is by winning."

Up and down the line, lords and captains were issuing the same instructions.

English Right Flank, 10:41 a.m.

"The French! The French come!" Warning cries rang along the right flank of the English army as lines of horsemen began to advance from the opposing French ranks.

"Make ready," the English captains roared.

Every archer checked his bow. Thick clumps of arrows, the heads planted in the soft earth, stood by each man. The grey and white feather flights resembled faded autumn flowers.

Robert Alderton stood in the front rank, studying the French horsemen. He had been given command of the right end of the English line with some five hundred archers. It was clear the enemy cavalry were going to try to turn the English flank, and the charge would come right through his men.

Alderton could see there were about a hundred riders. Far fewer than might have been expected, but even a handful of the armoured horsemen on their great chargers would inflict hideous carnage if they reached the archers.

The French horsemen were forming three lines with wide gaps between each rider to make it more difficult for the English bowmen to hit them. Alderton knew it meant that much of his force's fire would be wasted on empty ground, but the mounted men would still make excellent targets in their high-backed saddles that made it difficult for them to crouch or duck.

Alderton looked up and down the front line for any signs of panic: facing a cavalry charge could unnerve the most hardened soldiers. He was relieved to see that the line was still straight; none of the men was edging back.

At that moment the French spurred their mounts to a canter. Alderton knew they would be at full gallop after a hundred yards. He judged the distance; the French were two hundred and fifty yards away.

"Raise," he commanded.

With a single motion, five hundred men raised their longbows; the chisel-like arrow heads glinted darkly. Each man knew from experience the correct angle for the approaching target.

"Loose," thundered Alderton, bringing down his upraised right hand.

Five hundred bowstrings flew home in unison with a single splitting crack. Five hundred yard-long arrows soared heavenwards. A rush like beating wings filled the sky as the shafts' tail feathers parted the air.

The arrows hammered into the lines of enemy horsemen a second later. Many of the shafts thudded harmlessly into the mud; many bounced off the riders' helmets and armour; many were deflected by the iron plates and thick leather protecting the horses. But even the strongest armour has weaknesses, and gaps must be left so that men and horses can move, see and breathe. Dozens of arrows found such openings. Warheads sliced into the necks, wrists or knees of riders, and the backs of their horses.

Dead and dying steeds fell or swerved away; some cartwheeled, hurling helpless riders into the air.

Two volleys tore great gaps in the French lines, but the survivors kept advancing. Already they had covered more than half the distance to the English lines.

"Aim for their faces," Alderton shouted as his men drew their bows back a third time.

A few of the riders had not lowered their visors because they wanted to see better or had forgotten in the confusion. Arrows punctured their eyes or tore through foreheads and cheeks. Three arrows ripped into one knight's face simultaneously, the impact exploding his skull inside his iron helmet. Another arrow flew through the gaping mouth of a rider screaming a war cry, embedding itself in the back of his throat.

Men who had closed their visors were still buffeted or stunned as scores of arrows hammered at their helmets. Barely conscious, many tumbled from their saddles, the impacts breaking limbs and backs; riders following behind could do nothing as their terrified mounts pounded over the prostrate bodies.

More than three-quarters of the riders and horses were killed or injured in less than fifteen seconds. Scores of fallen men and mounts lay intertwined in heaps on the earth.

A handful of riders raced on towards the English. Guillaume de Saveuse, a knight said not to know the meaning of fear, won the honour of being the first Frenchman to reach the English lines that day. It was the last thing he ever did. Screaming with terror and pain from the two arrows protruding from its back, de Saveuse's battle horse charged blindly into a wooden stake. Its own momentum drove the jagged wooden point two feet into its chest. De Saveuse catapulted from the saddle, and was skewered on another stake. The dead horse stood rigidly still, propped up by the stake until the wood snapped a few seconds later under the animal's sagging weight.

Just two other French riders reached the English line. One was impaled on a stake when his horse was killed. The other tumbled unhurt from the saddle when an arrow brought his mount down. The rider lay half stunned on the ground until an archer brained him with a small iron axe. The bowman stood over the body until it stopped jerking. Satisfied, he spat on the corpse and returned to the ranks.

The few surviving horsemen pulled up short of the English, desperately trying to turn their confused and frightened animals around and flee. Alderton barked an order, and his men sprayed their backs with a final volley. Less than a dozen riders returned to the French lines.

"Hold!" Alderton stepped in front of the line, raising both his arms. "Save your arrows, lads. They'll be back soon enough."

English Left Flank, 10:42 a.m.

Things seemed to go better at first for the French horsemen on the other flank. Only half of the six hundred riders positioned there had wandered off during the long morning lull. As the trumpets sounded, some three hundred men-at-arms moved forwards to attack the English left flank. But while there were more of them, the riders were less eager to charge the English bowmen. Many of the French did not keep up as the formation advanced, and they turned back as soon as the archers opened fire. More men turned back when they saw the first casualties hitting the earth. Soon the retreating riders were colliding with the men behind them who were still trying to advance.

Only three horsemen reached the English lines on this side. A knight who had surged ahead alone was riddled with arrows as more than a hundred archers fired at him. The two other riders died seconds later in the same way.

"They're cowards!" exulted a young archer, pointing at the fleeing French. All around him men were laughing and slapping each other on the back; perhaps they might live to see another day.

"Silence," roared John Selby.

"Master Selby, we should rejoice. The French are beat!" the man cheerfully replied.

"Beat, is it, you squeaky bladder? There's much dying still to be done this day," Selby dourly retorted.

King Henry's Position, 10:46 a.m.

Henry had watched the destruction of the French cavalry. He had tensed as the first wave of horsemen charged the English right flank. Sheets of arrows obliterated the horsemen seconds later, cutting down men and mounts, and easing any doubts about the steadiness or skill of his bowmen.

"Sir Howard!" called Henry. "Attend me."

"Sire." Sir Howard Erpingham was standing unnoticed at the king's side. The knight was fifty-eight years old and had gone to war for the first time at the age of eleven. He had served in countless conflicts since, becoming one of the most trusted retainers of the king and his father before him.

"Forgive me. You are ever close at hand." Henry smiled.

"It will be so as long as I have breath to draw," Erpingham answered in his broad Norfolk tones.

"Are we within bow shot of the French army?"

Erpingham nodded. "It is some three hundred yards. A long shot, but the men can do it."

"Send orders for the archers to fire on your command. Concentrate their fire on the front ranks to inflict as many casualties as possible."

"We shall shower them with steel and break the dogs, sire," the knight said.

"It is more likely it will incite the French to attack."

"Then I will make sure that the men bring down as many as possible," Erpingham replied simply.

"I know you will, my old friend. And God be with you."

"May he be with us all, sire."

English Line, 10:48 a.m.

Orders raced along the English ranks to prepare for the attack. The royal clerks had told the king the night before that the wagon train contained half a million arrows. It seemed a huge number, but was only sufficient to equip each archer with a hundred arrows. If the men fired continuous volleys, they would run out of arrows after just ten minutes.

Captains shouted out commands to the archers to prepare to fire. The distance to the enemy lines meant the arrows would be losing momentum when they hit. Every ounce of strength would be needed if the warheads were to penetrate the French armour.

"Judge the range," captains and sergeants bellowed.

Five thousand men nocked yard-long shafts on their bowstrings, steadied themselves one last time, stiffening their backs to bear the strain.

"Draw." The command echoed up and down the lines.

With a single fluid motion, each archer pushed the yew stave forwards with his left hand, drawing the string back with the right. Each bow expanded into a great arc; it was the equivalent of lifting an iron anvil with a single hand. Five thousand men stood motionless, holding their bows extended in a steel-like grip despite the chest-crushing pressure.

Judging the moment perfectly, Erpingham dropped his upraised white baton. At the same moment every captain bellowed the order to fire.

"Loose."

Sheets of arrows hurtled into the sky as five thousand bowstrings tore home.

French First Division, 10:48 a.m.

With a mix of curiosity and dread, the French watched the wave-like motion as the English archers raised their bows. A moment later a black cloud soared upwards from the English lines. Some of those who survived would say later that it resembled a huge swarm of bees because of the angry, throbbing roar; others compared it to the wind stirring the trees just before a storm.

The French stared with fearful fascination as the black cloud hovered momentarily in the sky, and then plunged downwards. Less than a second later the stillness in the French ranks was shattered by the thunder of colliding steel and iron as thousands of arrowheads slammed into the tightly packed ranks of armoured men.

Every man caught in the deadly hail thought his last moment had come. Each one of them was hit at least once; many were struck many times. Most of the arrows spun off the armour, but hundreds found weak points, especially in the cheaper plate of the poorer men-at-arms. Jets of blood spurted from holes punched by the chiselled warheads; organs and bones exploded like ripe fruit as the barbs bit deep; some men died instantly, many more were wounded.

A second salvo tore into the packed mass of bewildered men seconds later. Screams of agony mixed with the roar of arrowheads hammering against armour. Some of the French stood rigid with terror. Others instinctively shielded their heads with their arms, only to be skewered in the elbow or wrist where the armour was weakest. A few tried to duck or evade the plummeting arrows, but any man who managed to dodge a shaft was immediately struck by two more. Some men had so many arrows protruding from them that they resembled monstrous birds with stunted feathers. Soldiers blindly pushed and jostled as the ranks turned into a heaving, terrified scrum. Blood gushing from the bodies of the dead and wounded formed deep pools.

English Lines, 10:50 a.m.

The English archers kept up the fire. The bowmen methodically loaded, aimed and fired. Captains shouted to check the range so that shots were not wasted.

King Henry's Standard, 10:50 a.m.

Standing in the centre of the English battle line, Henry watched the arrows raining down on the French. Gaps appeared in their ranks as men fell. Would it be enough, he wondered, to break them?

French Rear, 10:51 a.m.

David de Rambures, commander of the French crossbowmen, snarled with fury as he watched the English arrows raining down on the front ranks. A few salvos of crossbow bolts from his men would inflict terrible damage on the poorly protected English archers, and break up their attack. But the French lords had sent most of the crossbowmen home, saying they were not needed: the handful still on the field could only watch helplessly from the rear of the army.

His lieutenants listened as de Rambures cursed.

"At least we won't have to die on those hellish English arrows that skewer a man like a pig on a roasting spit," murmured one.

French First Division, 10:52 a.m.

Constable d'Albret gaped in disbelief at the slaughter around him. Arrows were blotting out the sky like snowflakes in a winter storm. Two of his bodyguards lay at his feet. One man was choking on an arrow protruding from his blood-filled mouth, the other was dead. Amid the screams of the dying and wounded, men beseeched Christ and his mother to save them.

D'Albret felt his head was spinning as he stared at the carnage and confusion. A ring of shouting men surrounded him – some demanding he order the army to attack, others imploring him to pull back. D'Albret could not see any of the other commanders. He struggled to think. Retreat would mean defeat and disgrace. Attack would expose the army to even greater slaughter as it marched straight into the English arrow fire. Either choice seemed impossible.

An arrow slammed into the front of d'Albret's helmet at that moment, bouncing off the steel plate; the impact was like a bone-shuddering punch in the face.

"Advance. Advance." He heard a voice shouting the order, and then realised it was his own.

Trumpeters sounded the command, the high-pitched calls rising over the shrieks of terrified and injured men. D'Albret pointed at the English lines with his sword, and took a step forwards. Twelve thousand armoured men lurched after him.

English Lines, 10:52 a.m.

The approaching French resembled a steel sea to the English, each line of men-at-arms a wave bristling with swords and lances. Awe mixed with fear in the minds of the watching English; it was a breath-taking sight, even if it might be the last thing they ever saw.

Sir John Cornwall watched the oncoming tide. In a lifetime of soldiering, he had never seen anything so terrible or majestic. Cornwall glanced at the men-at-arms of his contingent. Dread and disbelief contorted their faces.

"Steady, boys," Sir John rumbled in a deep voice. "We will give a good account of ourselves whatever else happens this day."

"Aye, Sir John. That we will," calmly answered Edward Banester. The hulking man-at-arms had fought by the knight's side for two decades, and had a sightless right eye and a limp to show for it.

Several of the other men nodded at his words, although most of them looked far from certain.

"A great and fearsome sight, Sir John," Banester muttered as they watched the approaching French. "Few men can have seen the like."

"Indeed, Edward. Although I hope the price of witnessing it is not too high."

"All men must die, Sir John, but there's not many that get to see death come striding across the fields for them."

Cornwall looked at the man. Banester was as calm as if they were sitting by the fire with tankards of ale on a winter's evening.

"I hope he does not come for you this day, my friend," the knight said softly.

King Henry's Standard, 10:52 a.m.

Fifty yards away, Henry continued to watch the French. The advancing formation was just a fraction of the French army, but it easily outnumbered his entire force. His gaze fell on the sword in his right hand: would it win or lose a crown in the coming hour?

English Camp, Maisoncelle, 10:52 a.m.

Thomas stood at the edge of the English camp trying to see what was happening on the battlefield. All he could make out were the sheets of arrows soaring across the sky from the English ranks. He could hear the hiss of the tail feathers, and the occasional blare of a trumpet, but it was impossible to tell how the battle was going.

Priests of the royal household were praying for the king and the army. Some jumbled the words as they struggled to control their fear; others chanted as if they were saying mass at home on a Sunday morning. Now and then one of the worshippers glanced up at the heavens, but none of them looked towards the fighting.

"Have you no duties to attend to, brother?" Esmond Lacy, the king's senior chaplain, approached Thomas.

"Your pardon, Brother Lacy. I was trying to see what is happening to the army," the monk explained apologetically.

"Why, are you needed there?" Lacy asked sternly.

Thomas crimsoned with embarrassment. He mumbled an apology.

"Brother," Lacy softened his voice, "we have our duties just as surely as the king and his soldiers have theirs. A battle is not a show of jugglers or bear baiters for children and idlers." The older man put his hand on Thomas' arm. "We shall know the outcome soon enough," he said. "Come. I will find you work to do."

French First Division, 10:54 a.m.

D'Albret glimpsed Boucicaut striding ten yards ahead. The marshal was at the front of the great mass of armoured men ploughing towards the English. Boucicaut wore a white surcoat emblazoned with a red eagle: the visor of his helmet was raised despite the arrows lashing the advancing ranks like rain, and he held a lance in both hands: he seemed not to have a care in the world.

Looking around, d'Albret realised the French advance was starting to break up as some of the troops surged ahead while others lagged; men were bunching together for protection from the arrow fire or huddling behind those in front. The division must stay intact and slam into the English like a giant wave all along their line; if it broke into straggling groups the enemy might be able to cut them down one by one.

"Boucicaut! Boucicaut!" D'Albret called. "We must keep the line straight! Keep the line straight!"

The marshal either did not hear or ignored the shouts. D'Albret cursed. What was the point? he thought. We will beat these English curs whether we do it neatly or like butchers.

Some of the French felt exhilaration or a savage joy as they surged forwards. Others stumbled like sleepwalkers, their minds and senses numb, carried along in the packed ranks. And there were more than a few who fell behind as fear burned their insides and shrill voices in their heads shrieked they were going to die.

Up ahead, dozens of horses paced nervously in the shrinking ground between the advancing French and the English battle line. Their riders had been shot from their backs in the failed French cavalry attacks. The frightened steeds bunched together for protection. Blood streamed from arrows embedded in the horses' flesh; every step or movement was agonising. The animals eyed the approaching army. Fearing being trapped, and blocked by the hedge of stakes in front of the English line, the horses suddenly bolted through the French.

Screaming soldiers were tossed into the air or crushed under the iron hooves. Some of the horses tripped and fell, snapping men caught under them like brittle twigs. Men tried to help friends who had been knocked down, but most of the troops pushed on blindly, trampling the helpless figures into the mud.

English Left Flank, 10:54 a.m.

Sheets of arrows flew from the English lines every five or six seconds. Each salvo of five thousand arrows tore great gaps in the French ranks, but they showed no sign of slowing. As they took aim, the archers could see the enemy bowing their heads and shoulders, like men caught in a storm.

John Selby could see that the archers were inflicting hideous casualties. As the French got closer, the arrows were finding more and more weak spots in the enemy troops' visors, neck pieces and leggings. But the English captain could see just as clearly that it was not enough. For every Frenchman who went down, twenty more seemed to take his place. And the enemy were now less than a hundred yards away.

"Aim for the faces!" he bellowed. "Hit them between the eyes!"

His sergeants took up the cry. Captains in other contingents echoed it. Aiming at a small target like a man's face would slow the rate of fire, but it was their best chance of breaking the enemy's will.

And a slower rate of fire might not be such a bad thing, Selby anxiously thought, as he saw how the thickets of arrows next to each archer were thinning out. A few more minutes, and his men would have nothing left to fire.

Second French Division, 10:55 a.m.

The duke of Alençon, who commanded the second French division, felt as if his heart was going to burst as he staggered forwards. All he could see through the tiny slits of his visor was a sea of mud. His feet slid on the greasy muck. His retainers grabbed his arms, stopping the duke from toppling head-first into the sludge.

Alençon had been stunned when the first division started off without warning. He cursed d'Albret and Boucicaut as his iron-clad feet sank into the bottom of the next furrow: why had they not told him they were attacking? His lieutenants had surrounded him, shouting and demanding action, as he gaped at the receding backs of the first division. Bewildered, he ordered his command to follow.

A carpet of bodies marked the progress of the men ahead. Arrows jutted from gaping wounds in some; others showed no sign of injury. Alençon ducked as a sheet of arrows hurtled out of the sky. A moment later the missiles struck helmets and armour with a roar like a thousand blacksmiths pounding on anvils.

"Help me, you fools," Alençon roared as he tried to step over a sprawling corpse. Two grunting retainers heaved the duke over the obstacle.

French First Division, 10:56 a.m.

The elation which had surged through the French ranks began to falter beneath the torrent of English arrows. More and more of the soldiers tried to avoid the murderous deluge by sheltering behind those around them. The French line began to shorten and pull in at either end as the division bunched together in the centre of the field; it only prolonged the exposure to the English fire by slowing the advance.

Most of the arrows bounced off the French armour, but it was still like being pelted with rocks. Men staggered each time they were hit; many were knocked to the earth, dazed or unconscious. Most clambered to their feet, but more and more were trampled under the iron legs of the men pushing from behind.

There had been just three hundred yards to cross when the advance began. Now it seemed that they would never reach the English lines.

Muscles and bones ached from the weight of armour and weapons as the soldiers staggered up the muddy slope. Panting men struggled to breathe inside their rib-squeezing armour and suffocating helmets; sweat streamed down faces, stinging their eyes and blurring their vision.

A full suit of armour weighed up to eighty pounds, two-thirds of a man's weight. The crippling load the soldiers had to carry was increased by the thick, heavy mud coating their iron-clad legs up to the thighs. Each step was an exhausting battle to wrench one foot from the clinging slime without losing their balance. Distances that should have been covered in seconds were consuming minutes because of the mud, the confusion in the tightly packed ranks, and the torrent of arrows.

The world blurred into nightmarish sights and sounds through the narrow slits of their visors: of soldiers pushing and shoving as they staggered forwards; the bellowed curses of terrified and angry men; clouds of arrows blotting out the sky; the shrieks of agony from the dying and wounded; and the growing carpet of corpses that had to be clambered over.

Still, the great armoured tide pressed forwards.

English Right Flank, 10:58 a.m.

"Captain! We need more arrows!"

Robert Alderton lowered his bow. The men around him were down to a handful of arrows. He saw one of the boys tasked to keep the archers supplied with new shafts from the supply train; there were tears in his eyes.

"There be no more, captain," the boy blurted. "I went to the wagons, but they are empty."

All of the archers looked anxiously at the captain. Hundreds of enemy bodies littered the ground, but the French were coming closer and closer.

"Steady, lads. Steady." Alderton gripped them with his voice. "Mark your targets. Make sure every shot counts. We'll get more arrows."

Obediently, the archers raised their bows and resumed firing.

Alderton's assurance had bought time, but he had no idea of how to make it come true.

King Henry's Standard, 10:59 a.m.

Sir Howard Effingham saw the slowing rate of fire from the archers and guessed the reason. He pushed his way through to where the king was standing beneath the red and white banner of England.

"Sire," he called anxiously.

Henry looked around as the knight approached. "I know," he responded before Effingham could say more.

The two divisions of French men-at-arms were rolling towards the thin English line. The enemy showed no sign of stopping despite the arrows cutting down row after row of men.

"At least we shall not have long to wait," Henry said.

French First Division, 11:00 a.m.

Boucicaut could see that the English line was less than fifty yards away as he pushed forwards. Miraculously, he had not been hurt by the English arrows, although he had received glancing blows several times.

Looking back, the marshal saw that the first division was disintegrating as the troops huddled together in a hopeless attempt to avoid the arrows. The long line, which had covered the entire English front when it started, had contracted into a confused mass in the centre of the field. The attack was bunching up even more as the men all tried to reach the opening in the wooden stakes where the English men-at-arms waited. The mud, the slope, the weight of their armour and the arrows raining down on the men's hunched heads and shoulders had slowed the French advance to a crawl.

It will not matter, Boucicaut thought, as long as we hit the English centre with enough force to break it. He could now see that the enemy men-at-arms were only four ranks deep. Gritting his teeth, he ducked his head and pushed on.

A moment later Boucicaut saw a wedge of men dash ahead. It was led by a knight in armour gleaming like silver. He recognised the lord of Croy and his companions. As if they were boys chasing a ball, the laughing young men urged each other on, racing to reach the English lines first. The fools will be cut to pieces, he thought, but they do not lack for bravery.

English Centre, 11:02 a.m.

The meagre lines of English men-at-arms tensed as the French surged over the last few intervening yards. The roar of thousands of screaming enemy soldiers engulfed them like breakers crashing on the shore.

Henry was clearly visible in the centre of the English line: the tip of the enemy advance seemed to be aimed straight at him. Some of his nobles had pleaded with the king not to fight in the first line; if he was struck down, they said, the battle would be lost in an instant.

Henry looked up and down the silent rows of English men-at-arms one last time. On the right, he could see York in his hulking suit of armour. Camoys stood beneath his gold and blue standard on the left. Gloucester stirred nervously behind him. Henry checked an impulse to turn and comfort his brother. All of us are afraid, he thought, and each of us must face our fears alone.

French Centre, 11:02 a.m.

Boucicaut levelled his lance at the face of an English man-at-arms. All around him French soldiers raised their swords, lances and poleaxes, tensing for the first exchange of blows when the two armies collided. They could see how few the enemy were. The fear and exhaustion which had gripped every man was replaced by savage confidence. Screaming for blood and revenge, the French stormed over the last ten yards.

The Armies Collide, 11:03 a.m.

A forest of spears and lances blotted out the sky as the French torrent crashed into the English centre. Hundreds of armoured bodies collided with a thunderous crack. War cries, curses and screams mingled with the clash of blades and lances hacking at helmets, armoured shoulders and breastplates.

The English centre staggered under the impact. The four lines of English men-at-arms compressed into a single slender belt of frantically struggling men. The French relentlessly pushed them. The English stumbled back, losing ground each second.

"They cannot hold," a French knight yelled triumphantly as he lashed at an English knight in a white surcoat emblazoned with black ravens. "Cut them down!"

Already the English had fallen back several yards: a few more steps and their line would break. Thousands of French men-at-arms pushed and shoved, trying to force their way to the front before all of the English were killed.

With a scream of triumph, the lord of Croy swung his sword into the neck of an English soldier, half tearing the man's head from the shoulders. He pushed forwards, bellowing Henry's name as his band of knights followed.

English Left Flank, 11:04 a.m.

John Selby aimed at a French man-at-arms two hundred yards away. The man jerked when the arrow whipped into his side; he clawed at the air as if seeking something to hold on to and then crumpled to the ground. Nocking a new shaft, Selby hunted for a fresh target. Shooting was more difficult now the French and English men-at-arms were locked in a confused mass in the centre of the field.

"Captain Selby," Thomas Downer called. "The boys say there are no more arrows."

Selby looked at the two urchins trailing behind the sergeant.

"They came back from the baggage wagons. They say there are no more arrows," Downer repeated.

Suddenly everything was going wrong. He could see the French were pushing back the centre of the English battle line. The fire of the English bowmen had dwindled to a trickle. The army was finished if the arrows were all gone.

A dozen men had heard Downer, and left their places in the line. Selby could see that none of them had arrows.

"Back to your posts," Selby snapped.

"How can we fight without arrows, captain?" whined a red-faced man. The front of his dun breeches were black; Selby realised the man had wet himself with fear.

"Get back to your places, and be silent," Selby thundered.

Reluctantly the archers returned to the firing line.

"Thomas." Selby motioned the sergeant to stay as the men trudged away. "Send the boys to the rear. No point in their being butchered with the rest of us."

King Henry's Standard, 11:05 a.m.

Henry parried a blow from a French knight. He swung his sword up, skewering the man under the chin. Fear and disbelief flashed across the knight's eyes as he died. The banners marking Henry's position were drawing the enemy like summer flies to a bloated corpse. Men tore at each other in a milling mass of bodies as fighting raged around the king.

It had become apparent within seconds of the armies colliding that the English had one advantage despite their far fewer numbers. The French had cut down their lances to make it easier to fight on foot, which meant the lances of the English men-at-arms were up to six feet longer. The English lances now formed a deadly fence on which the French were being slaughtered as they lunged uselessly at the empty air with their shorter weapons. But the weight of the thousands of French men-at-arms pushing forwards meant that some were breaking through as the English line buckled and occasionally splintered.

"Sir Thomas, look out!" Henry shouted. The elderly knight whirled about to see a French soldier with an upraised sword. Effingham stumbled backwards. In the same second, a royal guard thrust his spear into the lightly protected back of the Frenchman's thigh, sending him sprawling. A fountain of blood spurted from the gaping wound as the guard wrenched the lance free.

English Centre, 11:07 a.m.

The English centre bent under the ferocious French onslaught, and then steadied. Only a few hundred men could fight in the gap between the rows of wooden stakes where the two armies had collided. The massive French numbers were turning into a liability as the men in front were squeezed between the blades of the English and their countrymen blindly pushing from behind.

Constable d'Albret saw what was happening. Frantically he tried to stop the shoving herd of French soldiers. He lashed out with the flat of his sword, bellowing commands to stop. Men thought the constable had gone mad, others cursed him as they ducked or fended off the blows; none of them could hear his shouted warnings.

Sir John Cornwall's Detachment, 11:08 a.m.

Sir John Cornwall drove his mailed fist into the Frenchman's face; the man's nose exploded in a shower of blood and skin. A swift second punch caught the stunned man in the mouth, shattering his blackened teeth. Blinded by blood and mucus, the soldier staggered back, giving Cornwall room to thrust with his poleaxe. The spike rammed into the man's groin; shrieking with agony, the Frenchman fell.

"Kiss Satan's hairy arse for me!" the knight grunted as he drove the bloody spike into the convulsing body.

Cornwall's men-at-arms were locked in vicious struggles around him. The knight had never seen such savagery. Two men wildly stabbed at each other with daggers, both oblivious of their own wounds as they slashed and hacked. Another pair rolled in the mud, hands clamped around the other's throat. Shrieks of rage and hatred mingled with the cries of dying men and the clash of steel.

Seasoned fighters knew to aim for the armpit, elbow or other weak spots in an adversary's armour. Men in the strongest steel plate, able to withstand any sword or axe, could still be stunned by blows to the head or their swords and lances knocked from their hands, leaving them defenceless.

Blood covered everything. It poured from cuts and slashes, spurted from punctured armour, streamed down faces, chests and limbs. Glistening red puddles made the mud as slippery as ice; men slid and fell as they slashed and tore at each other.

King Henry's Standard, 11:10 a.m.

Henry saw the English line had steadied after the first shock of the French impact, and was pushing back. His men flailed furiously at the enemy, impaling opponents on the tips of their lances and poleaxes. But the French vastly outnumbered them, and the king could see a second wave of approaching enemy troops.

"For Saint George," he cried. The men around him took up the cry as they tore at the enemy.

Second French Division, 11:10 a.m.

The duke of Alençon roared at the chaotic mass of men around him to stop pushing and reform their lines, but if any of the soldiers could hear him amid the din they paid no attention. His command had caught up with the first division a moment before, but instead of sweeping away the English, they had only worsened the growing confusion. Up to twenty thousand pushing and shoving French troops were trying to reach the narrow opening where the enemy men-at-arms stood. Most of the French were hopelessly trapped in what had become a vast stationary crush of bewildered and angry men.

"Pull back!" Alençon screamed. "Form lines, you witless knaves!"

Other commanders also bellowed orders, trying to restore discipline; some cuffed and kicked the troops, but the attempts to impose order only added to the mayhem as the heaving mass of men blindly pushed at the English line.

Duke of York's Standard, 11:11 a.m.

The fiercest fighting raged around the standards of the English commanders, which drew hundreds of French fighters hungry for the glory of killing or capturing the greatest enemy nobles. A wedge of French men-at-arms flew at the duke of York's standard.

"Stop them!" York thundered as the attackers broke through his men.

Two household knights at the duke's side obediently dashed forwards. The duke, left alone, was rushed a moment later by three enemy soldiers. He floored one man with a savage sword blow. Desperately, York tried to wrench his blade free from where it had caught in the man's armour. With a howl of triumph, one of the other soldiers slashed at York's outstretched arms as he tugged at the sword. The cut bounced off the steel plate, but the blow numbed the duke's arms, knocking his hands from the hilt.

"Aid me! For God's sake, aid me!" he screamed.

No one heard the cry except the two French soldiers menacing him. York ducked to avoid a sword cut, only to pitch face-first to the ground when the second man tripped him with a lance. Howling with triumph, the French pounded on the duke's back with their weapons. The blows hammered the half-conscious noble into the muck like a tent peg. Liquid mud poured through the slits in his visor, surging into his nostrils and mouth.

The duke's guards killed the Frenchmen a minute later. By the time four of them had heaved the massive armoured figure from the mud and turned it over, the duke had drowned inside his mud-filled helmet.

English Right Flank, 11:12 a.m.

Robert Alderton watched as the second division of French troops joined the attack on the English centre. He could see the king's great standard with the red cross of Saint George, and the flags of the English nobles on either side. If just one of the flags fell, he knew it would mean the enemy had broken the English line. That would signal the end. The English men-at-arms would be cut down or captured. Then the French would turn on the archers, and they would show no mercy to the men who had slaughtered so many of their comrades.

Something had to be done, but the archers had exhausted their arrows. They could only stand and watch the fighting from behind the wooden stakes, their bows held uselessly at their sides.

"What must we do, captain?" a young archer called out.

"What can we do?" the man next to him said forlornly.

Glancing down, Alderton saw one of the wooden hammers used to drive the stakes into the ground. Without thinking, he bent and grasped the shaft, effortlessly raising the heavy tool, and strode towards the enemy as his puzzled men watched.

Alderton had gone ten yards before William Mason broke the silence.

"Master Alderton! What are you doing?" he yelled.

Without looking back, Alderton raised the hammer over his head and brandished it in reply.

The archers roared as they grasped his meaning. Half of them ran after him. The rest hesitated long enough to snatch up hammers, axes and anything else that would serve as a weapon. A moment later a wave of ragged, filthy men surged across the field.

Alderton steadied the hammer as he approached a French man-at-arms. The enemy soldier stared bewildered at the huge figure in a leather jerkin and green breeches. A moment later the hammer slammed down on the man's helmet, driving it into his skull. Alderton swung the hammer a second time, catching another French soldier on the side of the head; it exploded in a shower of grey brains and crimson blood.

Mason hurtled past Alderton to skewer a Frenchman with a long iron tent spike. He was followed by scores of shrieking archers who tore into the enemy, hacking at them with axes, hammers and spades.

Most of the French soldiers, intent only on pushing their way to the English centre, could not see the approaching archers. A few men on the fringes of the great mass of French troops shouted warnings. The cries were not heard by the men in the tightly packed crush. Only a few of the French turned to meet the attack.

One French knight caught a bowman on his lance, effortlessly driving the steel point through the man's wool shirt and deep into his chest. A moment later the grinning knight was floored by three howling archers. Two of the bowmen pinned the struggling knight by the arms as the third thrust a thin, rusty dagger through a slit in the helpless man's visor: pressing down with both hands, he rammed the needle-like blade through the shrieking knight's right eye, and deep into the brain.

English Left Flank, 11:14 a.m.

Archers on the left flank could see something was happening on the other side of the battlefield. One of John Selby's men clambered up one of the stakes for a better view; he perched at the end of the slanted log, balancing with outstretched arms.

"It's the Buckinghamshire men!" he called down.

"What are they doing?" Selby demanded.

"They are attacking the French. And they seem to be doing a right good job of it too," replied the man as he watched the distant melee.

"Now more of our men are joining in," he added.

"The archers on the other flank are attacking the foe?" Selby said doubtfully.

"Aye, Master Selby."

"Where in God's name did they get the arrows?" Selby demanded. "The boys swear the stores for the entire army are exhausted."

"Oh, they're not shooting, Master Selby," the archer distractedly replied as he peered across the battlefield.

Selby's hurled gauntlet caught the man on the side of his head, knocking him to the ground. He sprawled on the earth, struggling to comprehend what was happening, as the captain put a foot on his chest.

"What do you mean, they are not firing arrows, you mindless ox?" Selby spoke slowly, trying to control his anger.

"They are killing them with their hands," the archer groggily replied.

"What? Their hands?"

"Not their hands," the man corrected himself. "No, they are using those and such like." The archer pointed at one of the wooden hammers leaning against a stake.

Selby spun around. He could now see that the mass of enemy men-at-arms was being pushed back. Something or someone was stirring them up.

Selby unsheathed his sword. He had carried the weapon for twenty years, never once using it in combat. He pointed at the French with the outstretched blade.

"Grab whatever you can find to fight with, and follow me."

* * *

An archer dashed ahead as Selby strode towards the French. Without breaking his stride, the man bent and snatched a fist-size piece of flint from the ground. Swinging his arm, the bowman hurled it with unerring accuracy at an enemy spearman twenty yards away; the rock hit the man between the eyes, blinding him instantly.

"Eat that!" the archer screamed triumphantly.

Selby's yelling archers slammed into the stunned French seconds later. Soon the battlefield was covered with thousands of bowmen tearing at the enemy on both flanks. Hundreds of French soldiers were cut down as the archers brained them with mallets and clubs or slit their throats with jagged iron knives. Soon the French flanks started to buckle inwards as the English archers tore at them from both sides.

Selby saw two of his men rifling the body of a French knight: they had cut away the man's breastplate, and were shredding his shirt and vest for hidden jewels or money. Men took their valuables into battle rather than risk leaving them in their tents or the baggage train to be pilfered by camp followers.

"Stop, you witless varlets." Selby slammed the back of one man's head with his open hand. "Time enough for that if we live."

The pair grinned, snatched their discarded axes and ran to help the archers ringing a group of French men-at-arms. The encircled French held their own until an arrow split the face of the knight leading them. The knight toppled forwards as his horrified men gaped. A second later, another arrow thudded into the throat of one of the stunned French soldiers. With a howl of triumph, the archers rushed the survivors, felling them with a shower of blows from clubs and hammers.

Selby looked around to see where the shots had come from. Archers who had not discarded their bows were snatching arrows sticking up from the mud, and firing them into the huddled enemy ranks; at ranges of twenty yards or less, every barb was finding a target.

Not everything went the archers' way. The bowmen were not accustomed to this kind of fighting, and they were facing some of the finest soldiers in Europe. An archer seeing a solitary French knight closed for the kill. His grin turned to a grimace of astonished agony as the knight deftly thrust his sword through the archer's abdomen; it sliced through the man's guts before ramming into his spine. The knight placed a foot on the archer's shuddering chest, unhurriedly working the blade free from the sucking wound.

French Centre, 11:18 a.m.

Boucicaut reared back as an English man-at-arms swung at him with a sword. The tip of the blade scraped along the marshal's neck armour as it flashed past. One of Boucicaut's household knights lunged at the assailant with a lance. The Englishman swerved to avoid the thrust and stumbled backwards. With an exhausted grunt, the knight rammed the lance home.

Scores of similar contests were being fought out along the ragged line where the French vanguard heaved against the English centre. Arms were severed from torsos, heads cleaved to the teeth and men knocked senseless by blows from axes and maces. Stories and songs speak of two knights fighting for hours, exchanging hundreds of blows, but any man who has survived a battle knows most face-to-face contests are decided in seconds with no more than a blow or two.

Boucicaut could see that the English were winning too many of these combats. The enemy's smaller numbers gave them the edge in the narrow space where the armies were locked together; the English men-at-arms could move freely while most of the French were trapped helplessly in the milling mob behind the marshal. He cursed himself again for ordering the French army to shorten their lances; his men could only jab vainly at the empty air as the English picked them off with lances almost twice as long.

King Henry's Standard, 11:20 a.m.

With a howl of triumph, the lord of Croy charged the small band of men guarding the royal standard. Half of his band of young gallants had been killed fighting their way through the English line, but the survivors were still at his back.

"Henry! Henry!" Croy roared in heavily accented English.

Some of the king's guards heard the piercing screech. They braced, lances and swords extended. One lance half decapitated the knight just behind Croy: the spear point plunged into the man's screaming mouth, and his own momentum did the rest. Croy beat aside another thrusting lance and burst through the guards.

A tall figure stood beneath the flag. Croy saw the gold crown encircling the man's helmet. Three knights in red and blue surcoats with the arms of England guarded the man.

"Henry! Yield!" the Frenchman roared triumphantly. "Yield or die."

The king was staring at the right flank, trying to make out what was happening. He feared the enemy had broken into the English positions.

"Henry. Fight me!" Croy demanded.

The king whirled to see the Frenchman. Croy deftly ducked past the slashing blades of the three knights as they rushed forwards to engage the attacking French.

Visions of the glory and acclamation he would receive for killing the English king flashed through the young French lord's mind. Leaping forwards, he swung his sword down. Henry barely managed to block the blow. Croy lunged again, his blade hurtling at the king's head. Henry jerked away to avoid the cut, but it caught the side of his helmet. The blade snapped off one of the gold finials of the crown; it spun through the air. Henry staggered back. Sure of victory, Croy lunged a third time, but misjudged the distance, and the blade found only empty air. Henry caught the Frenchman with a savage blow to the back of the head as he hurtled past. Croy fell headlong. An English knight pushed past the king and rammed a lance deep between Croy's sprawling legs. Croy's back arched as he shrieked with agony; a second later his body went rigid and then slumped as death took him.

Henry was ringed by guards once again. All of Croy's band lay dead beneath the English banners fluttering overhead.

French Rear, 11:25 a.m.

"What is happening?" demanded the count of Dammartin. "Have they finished the English off?"

Thousands of men were milling about in the centre of the battle-field, but it was not clear if the French forward divisions had stalled or had overrun the English and were now finishing them off.

The count of Fauquembergue, who shared command of the French third division of some three thousand mounted men with Dammartin, was also peering at the swirling throng almost a mile away.

"We have closed with the enemy," he remarked.

"Clearly!" Dammartin snorted derisively. "Is it all over, yet? And what is happening on the English flanks? Men are moving about there."

Fauquembergue did not answer. Relations between the two nobles had soured from the moment they were handed joint command of the third division. Each man believed he alone should lead the horsemen who were to sweep down when the English broke, and finish off any enemy survivors who attempted to flee.

"If only d'Albret or Boucicaut would send word," Dammartin complained. "How do they expect me to act if they don't keep me informed?"

"Us," Fauquembergue coldly corrected him. "Keep us informed."

Dammartin shrugged irritably. "Very well. What do you suggest?"

Fauquembergue hesitated. "Perhaps the attack on the English rear will shake things up," he ventured. The battle plan called for a small force of local men to attack the enemy from behind.

"Attack!" Dammartin snorted. "Those men are just a rabble of peasants. God knows what d'Albret was thinking of when he dreamed that scheme up."

"Well, you keep saying the English are just peasants and scum, but surely French scum is better than the English kind, my dear count." Fauquembergue gurgled with pleasure at his clumsy joke.

King Henry's Standard, 11:26 a.m.

"They break! They break!" the duke of Gloucester screamed as the English men-at-arms pushed forwards against the French. "Hack them down!"

The enemy front ranks, exhausted from the advance across the fields and the ensuing hand-to-hand fighting, were wavering. Sensing triumph, the king's younger brother led his retinue in a charge that drove a wedge into the French line.

Humphrey had seen Henry cut down half-a-dozen Frenchmen. He was determined not to be outdone once again. He hacked at the head of an enemy soldier already on his knees. One of his knights blocked a French man-at-arms trying to spear the duke. Humphrey laughed. He would turn the tide of battle and lead the army to victory.

The duke was too busy with thoughts of his triumph to see the armoured figure pushing towards him in the melee of struggling men. The duke of Alençon had recognised Humphrey's coat of arms. His men cut down three English soldiers as Alençon hurled himself at Humphrey. The Englishman parried Alençon's sword cut; he did not see the dagger in his opponent's left hand. As Humphrey raised his sword to strike, Alençon gripped him around the chest with one arm and thrust the dagger up under the Englishman's breastplate and pierced the flesh. Humphrey screamed and staggered back, fighting to breathe.

Henry saw his brother fall. A moment later, the king was standing over Humphrey, fending off the blows of Alençon and three other Frenchmen. Henry's guards pushed forwards, forming a defensive line in front of the king and his brother.

A knight of the royal household helped Henry raise Humphrey's visor. The duke was barely conscious. Henry saw the blood seeping from his brother's waist.

"Get help. Take him to the camp," he commanded. A second knight helped lift the duke; a third man cleared a way through the English soldiers.

"Henry," Humphrey pleaded as he was lifted. "Please don't send me away."

The king did not answer. Briefly, he wondered if he would ever see the boy again. The battle was still in the balance.

Looking up, Henry saw his guards had beaten Alençon to the ground. He knelt on the mud ringed by English men-at-arms.

Henry strode towards the crouching Frenchmen. Alençon immediately recognised Henry by his crown and the royal arms on his surcoat.

"Sire, I yield to you," he called, raising his sword to give it to the king. A royal guard, mistaking the gesture as an attack, drove his battle axe into the back of the Frenchman's neck.

"But I yield," said Alençon in a puzzled voice before toppling in the mud.

English Right Flank, 11:26 a.m.

Robert Alderton's chest heaved with exertion. His hands, face and chest were red with the blood of enemy soldiers. He had lost count of how many Frenchman he had killed. All around him the English archers were attacking the French. Only the men on the fringes of the great mass of enemy troops were fighting back; unaware of the threat on their flanks, the tightly packed French men-at-arms continued to press blindly towards the English centre. Packs of bowmen cut into the French like wolves attacking a herd of deer, knocking the armoured men to the ground and hacking the life out of them. A few of the French tried to surrender, but the archers either did not understand or did not care, and slaughtered them.

Some of the archers, intoxicated by success, became careless. Alderton grimaced as a bowman armed only with knife rushed an enemy knight. The Frenchmen lopped off the archer's hand with a flick of his sword, and then severed the bowman's head from the shoulders as the stupefied man gaped at the red stump where his hand had been.

English Camp, 11:26 a.m.

Thomas kept looking up from the stores he was checking. The roar of thousands of men, the clash of weapons and the blare of trumpets carried across the fields, but he could see nothing of the battle.

The baggage wagons were ringed in a loose protective circle around the English camp. Scores of servants, clerks and grooms milled or sat about; most had nothing to do. Just ten men-at-arms and twenty archers had been left to guard the camp – all the king could spare. Thomas saw at least half of the guards had vanished; he guessed they had gone to join the battle. He wondered how long it would be before the others slipped away.

Angry scenes had flared when boys sent from the battlefield for arrows were told there were no more. Some of the lads cried, saying the king and his men would be killed; others cursed the storekeepers in angry, high-pitched voices.

Would that Christ was here to do another miracle like that with the loaves and fishes, Thomas thought.

"Brother," Esmond Lacy, who was working beside him, interrupted his thoughts. "There appear to be wounded."

Several men approached the camp; some staggered along, others were carried by companions.

"Go to the infirmary, Brother Thomas. Some of those poor souls may require the services of a priest," Lacy quietly ordered.

French Centre, 11:28 a.m.

D'Albret shouldered his way back through the throng of soldiers pressing against the English centre. A knight, thinking that the constable was running, held up a hand, blocking his passage.

"Coward! You lead us here and then run!" the man screamed.

"I am not running away, you fool!" d'Albret retorted. It was too late; the man had elbowed past without hearing. D'Albret rebuked himself; he was the constable of France, answerable only to the king.

D'Albret continued to shove his way through the crush of men; he had left the front after hearing confused shouts that the

English were attacking in the rear, which hardly seemed possible. A moment later d'Albret was able to see that the English archers were attacking the flanks of the horde of French troops stalled in front of the English centre. The confused, exhausted French soldiers were not turning to meet the threat.

"You!" D'Albret pulled at the shoulder of a passing soldier. "Form a line," the constable yelled, pointing at the attacking archers.

The man turned to look at him. Dark brown eyes gazed uncomprehendingly at the constable as if he was a phantom in a dream.

"We must turn to face them –" the constable gestured again at the archers – "or the army will be slaughtered."

The man shook off d'Albret's hand and trudged on. D'Albret was astonished. Did the man not see the threat. Two more soldiers walked past, also ignoring his pleas.

English Left Flank, 11:30 a.m.

John Selby caught the French man-at-arms a massive blow to the head with the wooden hammer. He was amazed when the Frenchman groggily staggered away. Selby shrugged and let him go: a man with such a hard head deserved to live. Very few of the French were getting second chances. Wild with blood and hate, the English bowmen slaughtered their far better armed opponents.

Some of the archers had found a new way to restock their quivers. Selby saw a tall bowmen lean over a wounded Frenchman lying on the ground; an arrow jutted from the man's convulsing chest. The archer placed a foot on the man's rib cage to keep him still before carefully working the shaft out as the soldier shrieked with agony. Holding the arrow up, the bowman carefully inspected the bloody head for damage; satisfied, he slipped the shaft into his quiver, lifted his foot and moved to another body.

"Get him!" Selby pointed at a French knight trying to slip away after feigning death among a clump of corpses. Two of his men tore after the fugitive; the knight ran only a few steps before slipping in the mud. One of the archers rammed the man's helmeted head deep into a brown puddle, pressing it down with his knee. Bubbles of air from the drowning knight broke the surface, and then he went limp. The smiling bowmen nodded cheerfully to Selby as they loped back to the fighting.

English Camp, 11:32 a.m.

William Bradwardyn inspected the injured man's shattered jaw. The left side of the soldier's face had been smashed by a blow from an axe or a mace; shattered teeth and jagged bone shards glinted amid the raw red flesh.

"Hold him. Take care not to cut off his breathing," the surgeon instructed Thomas and two of his own men. The man-at-arms was laid out on planks stretched across two barrels.

Bradwardyn began carefully to cut away bits of mangled flesh with a small razor. Blood welled around the glinting blade as he dug out a half-broken tooth. The man shrieked and lost consciousness.

Thomas watched fascinated as the surgeon's slender fingers carefully probed and cut, skilfully extracting fragments of bone and tooth. His curiosity seemed to have overcome his earlier nausea.

"You bear this well, Brother Thomas," Bradwardyn murmured as he searched the wound.

Surgeons worked on other wounded men stretched out on makeshift tables. Rows of gleaming knives and steel probes lay neatly on strips of white linen by each table. Straw was strewn nearby for the wounded to lie on. Feet protruded from a tarpaulin on the other side of the clearing where those the surgeons had not been able to save lay in a row.

* * *

"Look! The French!"

Bradwardyn did not look up from the wound he was probing. "Quiet," he muttered irritably.

"Sir, you don't understand! The French are attacking!" one of his assistants cried.

This time the surgeon glanced up. A hundred yards away, howling French peasants armed with pitchforks, scythes and clubs streamed through gaps in the circled wagons; three mounted knights led them.

The attackers literally ran over the handful of English guards. A few of the camp followers tried to fight, flailing at the French with kitchen knives or frying pans. A muscular priest swung a beer barrel over his head at two assailants – the spinning cylinder knocked both men sprawling.

"Kill them!" Ysembart d'Agincourt urged the mob on as he watched from his horse.

D'Agincourt was lord of the nearby manor. He had been ordered to attack the camp of the English with a handful of men-at-arms and six hundred peasants. D'Agincourt was far from happy with the task; he had gloomily told his cousin that there was no glory or honour in leading churls to war.

At least the fighting was proving far easier than d'Agincourt had expected. Most of the English were too old or too young to do anything but die. He watched an English cook holding off a dozen assailants with an iron roasting spit. Three serving-boys, none of them older than ten, cowered at his back. One of the French peasants lunged at the cook. The cook stabbed wildly, missing the man, who careened into him, knocking them both to the ground. The other peasants trampled over the intertwined bodies and encircled the boys. The oldest tried to shield his two companions until a peasant drove both spikes of a pitchfork deep into the child's stomach. Howling with triumph, the man raised his shrieking victim on the end of the fork, the boy's legs kicking wildly in the air. A dozen rough, horny hands tore at the two younger boys, scratching and raking their faces. A blow from a club brained one child while a rotund peasant gutted the smallest boy with a kitchen knife.

Thomas jerked back as a howling peasant slashed at him with a scythe. The long, curved blade just missed his throat. Cursing, the peasant swung the tool back for a second swipe. The monk darted away before he could strike.

Most of the English surgeons and their assistants lay dead and wounded around the operating tables where they had gone on working until the French stormed into the infirmary. Bradwardyn had plunged his scalpel into the eye of an attacker before ducking beneath the table. A peasant with a club brained the wounded English soldier the surgeon had been operating on.

Defenceless men were cut down and killed wherever Thomas looked. He watched, horrified, as two peasants pinned the arms of one of the English surgeons and a third selected a knife from the row of instruments on an operating table. Slowly, the man severed the screaming surgeon's throat, working the blade in and out of the taut flesh as his companions guffawed.

Thomas turned to flee, only to blunder into the peasant with the scythe. The man grinned malevolently as he raised the blade. A sword seemed to flash out of nowhere and block the descending scythe. Stunned, Thomas saw the French knight de Gaucourt skewer the peasant.

"Run!" De Gaucourt pointed to a nearby clump of beech trees. The two men fled, flattening themselves a moment later behind the broad trunks.

"You saved me." Thomas struggled to speak.

"And that baffles you?" De Gaucourt did not take his eyes from the English camp as he spoke.

Thomas peered over the knight's shoulder. He saw bodies littering the ground, and whooping peasants sacking the wagons.

"Forgive me, sir. I owe you my life. And yet I do not understand. You are French. An enemy of England," Thomas persisted.

"Always you ask questions, brother." De Gaucourt looked at him. "Why don't I kill you and join these savages in the slaughter? Because I am a true knight, and a man of honour. I do not kill children or the innocent. Now be silent or we will both die."

Jubilant peasants looted the wagons, trampling over the dead and dying bodies of the English. Hoots of joy rang out as they tore open bales and boxes, revealing rich clothing, weapons and other possessions.

D'Agincourt swiped with the flat of his sword at a peasant pawing a small wooden box. The blow caught the man on the back of the head, sending him staggering back. Enraged, he raised a club, only to lower it immediately when he saw d'Agincourt.

"Clear off, pig." The knight brandished the naked blade. "There's plenty of swill for you elsewhere."

Nodding numbly, the man retreated backwards several steps before turning and running.

D'Agincourt peered into a wagon. It was a finely carved vehicle, sitting high on four wheels. It must be the English king's carriage, he marvelled. At that moment his cousin looked out of the gaping doors. He held a gold crown in his outstretched hand.

"You won't believe it. There are jewels and money. All the treasure of England is here," the man babbled. "Oh, and I found this."

The man held up the finest sword d'Agincourt had ever seen. Its great hilt was gold, and it glinted with jewels; the blade was encased in a rich red velvet scabbard adorned with golden lions.

"It is their king's sword of state, the symbol of his power," d'Agincourt gasped.

French Centre, 11:32 a.m.

Panic spread through the trapped French troops. Thousands of the men who had surged forwards on foot to attack the English lines less than an hour earlier lay dead or wounded. The tired survivors were being driven into an ever smaller crush of tightly packed bodies as their will to fight seeped away.

D'Albret could see many of the soldiers were close to breaking. He knew that what would start as a trickle would explode into a rout if the men tried to flee to the French lines. There would be a massacre as the English pursued them. The men just need to be led, and they will fight, he thought. At least his trumpeter was still with him.

An English archer less than a hundred yards away heard the piercing call. He saw a man with an upraised trumpet in the throng of French soldiers. The archer watched as a lord seemed to give commands to the milling soldiers. Wonder what he's saying, the archer thought, raising his bow.

The arrow plunged into d'Albret's forehead just as he was calling out that the battle was not lost.

English Right Flank, 11:34 a.m.

Robert Alderton wondered if he might live to see another day after all. Everywhere he looked, archers hacked down the enemy with axes and clubs. It had become a game for some of the men: they laughed and jeered as the demoralised French shrank back.

Some of the English were allowing the French to surrender now that victory seemed to be theirs. A knight had offered Alderton his sword, and then a lord had yielded with six of his retainers. The little group of prisoners stood silently behind him under the guard of two of his men. He hardly dared think of the fat ransoms they would bring, and how it might transform his life and that of his family.

Alderton watched warily as three archers approached. The man in front gripped knives in both fists; he seemed to be wearing long red gauntlets. It was only when he got closer that Alderton saw the man's arms were stained crimson with blood to the elbows.

"All is well. These men are my prisoners," Alderton called out.

The man with the knives stared at the prisoners with eyes resembling glistening black pebbles; there was no feeling or emotion in them.

"Prisoners," the man mumbled as if he had never heard the word before.

"They have yielded, and will fight no more," Alderton cautiously answered.

The man seemed even more puzzled. "They be French?" he asked in a voice hoarse from screaming.

"Aye," the captain answered.

"Then we must kill them," the man said. He and his companions stepped forwards, eying the prisoners like butchers sizing up pigs in a market pen.

The captain put a hand on the archer's shoulder; the man looked at it, puzzled, and then at Alderton.

"No, lad. They have yielded. It is not right to kill prisoners," Alderton spoke gently as if explaining to a child.

"But they are French. The king says we must kill the French." There was no hint of anger or any other emotion in the man's voice.

"King Henry would not wish us to kill defenceless men."

For a minute, the archer stared blankly at the prisoners. Suddenly, he shrugged and turned.

"Come. There are plenty of other buggers to kill," he told his companions.

"What was wrong with him, captain?" one of Alderton's men asked. "Was he a lunatic?"

"Of a kind. He has the killing rage. It has driven him half out of his mind."

French Centre, 11:35 a.m.

Marshal Boucicaut wearily swung the poleaxe, forcing back the English swordsmen. One of his knights parried a blade as it flew at Boucicaut's head; the marshal had lost count of how many times his life had been saved that day by his retainers.

Wherever he looked, the French army was falling back under the English onslaught into an ever tighter and more helpless mass of men. The English men-at-arms were driving the French back from the front as their archers tore into both flanks. The living trod on the dying and the dead as they lashed at each other.

Boucicaut had started the day with twenty battle-hardened retainers. Two were still standing. Grief gripped him. How had this happened? he wondered. How could the finest army France had sent to war in generations meet such a fate at the hands of a miserable rabble just a fifth of its size?

"Saint Denis save us!" he roared as the English closed in led by a huge man. Boucicaut jabbed at the towering figure. The giant knocked the poleaxe down with his sword and grasped the shaft with his other hand before Boucicaut could react.

Laughing, the Englishman tossed his sword aside and then, hand over hand, pulled the poleaxe in. The marshal knew he should let go, but he clung to the weapon: he could feel one of his knights tugging at his shoulders, pleading with him to let go.

Boucicaut stared blankly at the grinning giant; his visor was raised. He could make out each of the man's yellowing teeth, and a thick tongue that seemed to shake with laughter. A moment later the man's hands closed over his in an iron grip.

"Yield. You are my prisoner."

Boucicaut heard the words as if they were coming from far away. He was mildly surprised that the giant was speaking French. A man collapsed by his side. Looking down he saw the retainer who had tried to pull him back; the man was dead.

"Yield!" the giant yelled a second time.

With a last surge of strength, Boucicaut yanked his right hand free and reached for the hilt of his sword. He had the blade half out of the scabbard before the Englishman knocked him sprawling. An English man-at-arms slammed an iron-shod foot down on Boucicaut's face, smashing his nose; blood filled the marshal's eyes.

"Enough," Sir Gilbert Umfraville ordered. "Leave him."

King Henry's Standard, 11:36 a.m.

Henry could see the French giving ground everywhere. English men-at-arms and archers tore at the enemy, many of whom huddled trapped and unresisting, unable to evade the blows.

"Keep at them," he cried.

The men around him heard the king's command, and cheered. Up and down the line, the English hacked and hewed at the enemy with the fury of men turning on their would-be executioners.

French Rear, 11:40 a.m.

"Good God, I can't believe it!" the count of Dammartin exclaimed. "Some of our men seem to be falling back. We must act."

"Impossible!" declared the count of Fauquembergue. "They must be wounded leaving the fray."

Both men peered over their horses' heads. French soldiers straggled back over the fields singly and in small groups. Fighting was raging behind them where the armies remained locked together.

"Why doesn't d'Albret send word?" Dammartin complained. "He must tell us what to do!"

"I imagine the good constable is a trifle preoccupied," Fauquembergue drily replied.

"Our own men won't stand much more of this," Dammartin muttered. "Half of them look as if they're ready to run."

Fauquembergue looked over his shoulder at the hundreds of mounted men waiting in loose lines. Confusion, apprehension or resentment was apparent on many of their faces.

Movement on the road caught Fauquembergue's eye at that moment. "What's this?" he said.

"Riders!" one of the soldiers shouted. "It must be reinforcements!"

Hundreds of men looked where the man was pointing. A dozen horsemen were cantering along the track from Agincourt.

"Precious few reinforcements," Fauquembergue said.

Anthony, duke of Brabant, rode up to the two counts. His face was smeared with sweat and dirt from hard riding; his horse's chest heaved, and steaming foam coated the animal's muzzle.

"I am Brabant," the duke curtly introduced himself. The two counts inclined their heads just enough for the gesture to be seen. Brabant was the younger brother of the duke of Burgundy, the powerful rival of the king of France. Burgundy had ignored the crown's pleas for aid, happy to let the English and French tear each other apart. He had, however, allowed some of his followers to fight for the French king as emotions against the English rose across France.

"Welcome, your grace," Dammartin greeted the young noble.

"Why do you sit here while the rest of your army fights?" Brabant curtly demanded.

Dammartin reddened and began to protest. Fauquembergue put a hand on his arm to silence him.

"Your grace perhaps does not understand the situation," Fauquembergue said.

"I see your army is locked in battle while you sit here with a large force of horse doing nothing," the duke snapped.

"Perhaps if your grace had come a little sooner, he would know the commanders of the army gave explicit instructions that we hold this position until the English break," Fauquembergue shot back. "Is this your grace's entire force?" he continued with mock-surprise.

Brabant glared at Fauquembergue. "We have ridden thirty miles since dawn. Most of my men are strung out along the road behind us," he replied. "It may be hours before they are all here."

"Your grace is most welcome whether he comes alone or at the head of an army," Fauquembergue's tone suggested otherwise.

"Enough! We are not playing games at court!" Brabant raised his voice. "Your army is clearly in trouble. You must attack!"

Dammartin hurriedly intervened, "The situation is difficult, your grace. We are not sure what is happening."

Brabant pointed at the fighting across the field. "Who are those wild men who tear at the flanks of your army?"

"We are not sure. It may be the English archers. A disgusting peasant rabble," Dammartin explained.

"Low-born or not, they appear to be getting the better of your well-bred gentlemen," the duke said.

The two counts glared at the younger noble.

"My lords," Brabant forced himself to speak calmly. "I appeal to you. Can you not see that we must act before all is lost?"

"We have our orders," Fauquembergue coldly replied. "I can do nothing."

Brabant struggled to master his fury. He turned to Dammartin. "Sir, will you ride with me against the English?"

Dammartin looked at Fauquembergue for help, who remained silent, and then back at the duke.

"Your grace, perhaps it is best we wait until the situation is clearer," Dammartin pleaded.

"Wait! Your army is dying and you want to wait!" Brabant spun his horse around to face his small band of attendants. "Where is my armour?" he ordered. The Burgundians, not expecting to blunder into the middle of a battle, wore only riding clothes.

"It is still with the baggage, your grace," one of his knights said. "The wagons will not be here before nightfall."

"Who will give me armour?" Brabant demanded.

"I have a few pieces in my saddlebags, sir. It would be better if you wait until the rest of our force arrives," another of the Burgundians answered.

"There is no time. Help me arm."

Brabant slid from his horse. Two attendants hurriedly helped the duke don a breastplate and helmet. The helmet was at least a size too small and pressed uncomfortably against his head.

"Wait. You do not have your surcoat." One of his men anxiously pointed at Brabant's bare breastplate. Chivalry required that a knight display his coat of arms in battle.

"Sir, will you lend me your colours?" Brabant gestured at the pennant on the lance of one of the French men-at-arms.

"It would be an honour, your grace."

171

The man lowered his lance. With a nod of thanks, Brabant slit a hole in the pennant before slipping it over his head. It hung crookedly on his borrowed armour.

"Follow me, anyone who still has honour." Flinging a final taunt at the French leaders, Brabant spurred his mount forwards.

French Centre, 11:44 a.m.

Brabant lowered his lance as he kicked his nervous horse to a full gallop. Six of his riders followed him: none wore full armour, and only three had helmets. Brabant rode past French men-at-arms straggling back from the battle.

"Fight, you cowards," he roared. None of the men paused or looked up as the little band of Burgundian horsemen thundered by.

"Charge!" the duke yelled as he spotted a group of English archers. Hunching low over his lance, he charged. An arrow caught the duke's horse in the chest before it had covered ten yards; it pitched forwards, flinging its rider like a stone from a catapult. A second later a salvo of arrows knocked his followers from their saddles.

"Fools," muttered William Mason as he nocked an arrow on his bow. "These French never learn."

French Centre, 11:45 a.m.

Frightened and exhausted French troops staggered through the mud, trying to escape the carnage. What had begun as a trickle back to the original French lines was turning in to a torrent. Men stumbled and fell over the bodies and weapons that littered the ground.

Screaming packs of English archers darted between the fleeing French. Some of the archers yelled or laughed as they plunged swords and knives into the helpless enemy; others worked methodically, cutting and slicing with no more than an occasional grunt of exertion.

An elderly French lord tried to weave his way through the clumps of brawling men as he staggered towards the French rear. Guillaume de Martel had lost his sword, but he still clutched the Oriflamme standard. He stumbled through the mud, using the flagpole as a staff to stay upright. The red banner, raised before the battle to show that the English would receive no mercy, flapped uselessly over his bent head.

De Martel glanced up. He could see lines of French horsemen at the far end of the battlefield. Gasping, he raised himself and lurched onwards. He did not hear the man behind him or the descending club that knocked him senseless to the ground.

De Martel was unconscious when the archer rolled him on to his back.

"What's that funny thing," said the archer's companion, looking at the red banner half hidden beneath the prostrate nobleman. "Think it's worth anything?"

"Nah. Just a bit of tatty old cloth," the other replied. "Old fool should have stayed at home by the fire."

Crouching over the body, the man slit the French lord's throat, and then carefully wiped the blood from his dagger on a corner of the flag.

French Centre, 11:56 a.m.

The English had almost surrounded what was left of the two French divisions. Dead and wounded littered the ground. Some of the corpses were horribly disfigured: heads cleaved in half, limbs hacked off, purple and grey entrails protruding from split torsos. Other bodies showed little or no sign of injury: many men had suffocated in the mud or been knifed through the eye, groin or other weak points in their armour.

Among the butchered bodies, groups of French knights and men-at-arms fought on, lashing at the encircling English. Others were too tired to fight: they stared blankly, not resisting as the English finished them off.

Sir John Cornwall caught the arm of an archer about to dispatch a Frenchman kneeling at his feet. The archer snarled, trying to free his arm.

"No, lad." Cornwall soothed. "Leave him."

The archer looked bemused for a moment, and then freed his grip on the Frenchman with a shrug.

Cornwall studied the crest on the prisoner's soiled white surcoat. "As I thought – the duke of Orleans," he said.

Only then did Cornwall see the tears streaking the captive's cheeks, and the lips quivering with fear. The duke's armour showed no sign of combat.

"Please, I beg of you. Do not kill me." The man who had derided the other French leaders for cowardice grovelled at the Englishman's feet. "I am rich. I will give you money."

"This is shameful," Cornwall's voice turned sour. "Try to act like a noble even if you are not a man."

French Centre, 12:03 a.m.

More and more French soldiers were being allowed to surrender as the killing fury of the English subsided. Soon several thousand had been taken captive and herded together in front of what had been the English battle line. The French removed their helmets and gauntlets and laid down their weapons to show they had yielded. English archers rifled the enemy dead for jewels and money. Several great French lords were discovered lying injured or trapped under piles of bodies.

The duke of Brabant was found sprawled unconscious in front of his dead horse. An archer called out to an English knight.

"Sir, be this a great lord worth his weight in gold?" the man asked hopefully.

The knight looked at the borrowed pennant around Brabant's neck. He noted the mismatched and incomplete bits of armour on the fallen figure.

"That's not a coat of arms. Looks as if the fool thought he could pretend to be a lord by purloining some armour and draping that rag around his neck. He is nobody."

"Pity, that," the archer muttered good-naturedly as he raised an axe to finish off one of the greatest lords in France. "The old woman would have been right pleased if I'd come home with a pot of gold."

King Henry's Standard, 12:17 p.m.

Henry surveyed the carnage littering the ground. One moment men had been hacking and clawing at each other, screaming with hate and fear, and then suddenly there was silence. His exhausted soldiers stared at the corpses blanketing the earth; a man could not move in the centre of the field without treading on a body.

A line of French captives was led past as the king watched. The prisoners shuffled along, staring dejectedly at the ground, mute from weariness and shock. His own men wandered across the field in small groups or alone. The English seemed as stunned as the French by what had happened.

"I have never seen such sights." Awe mixed with horror in Camoys's voice. "God and his angels will weep to see such things."

Henry looked at the man standing beside him. There was not a trace of the usual irony or scorn in the old man's expression.

"It is Heaven's will," the king said.

Camoys was silent for a moment as if he could not comprehend Henry's words.

"Yes. It must be so," he murmured. "How else could such a thing happen."

"Sire! Sire!" A knight of the royal household broke the silence. "This monk brings grievous news."

Henry looked at the tall figure beside the knight. He was deathly pale; his cassock was coated with blood. The king immediately recognised him.

"Brother Thomas, are you hurt?"

Thomas looked confused for a moment, then saw the gore staining his chest.

"Oh. No, it is not mine," he stammered. "The blood, I mean."

"Thank Heaven, brother. What has happened?" the king asked. "Tell me."

"They are all dead. All dead," Thomas' voice cracked.

Henry could see the monk was near collapse.

"Who is dead, brother," he asked softly.

"Everyone." Thomas stared dejectedly at the ground. "We had no warning, and the guards were too few."

"Was this at the camp?" Henry asked patiently.

"The French attacked from the rear, sire. There were so many of them. They cut down the guards, and then they killed the servants, the clerks and everyone else. Even the youngest boys. They killed them all."

The listening men gasped, still capable of being horrified despite what they had seen that morning.

"Are the French still there?" Henry coaxed.

"No, sire. They sacked the camp and fled."

"How is it you are alive?"

"The French knight, de Gaucourt. He saved me," Thomas said.

"And this?" Henry gestured at the blood smearing the monk's robes.

"One of the boys was still alive. I held him in my arms, but I could not save him."

Henry put a hand on the sobbing monk's shoulder.

"You gave comfort when every man needs it the most," he said. The king turned to the knight who had brought Thomas. "Protect him," he ordered.

At that moment Henry saw movement in the large formation of French horsemen on the other side of the fields. Were they preparing to attack? he wondered. His army was scattered across the battlefield. They would be helpless if the French cavalry attacked or the force that had sacked the camp appeared again in the rear. And the thousands of French prisoners might seize the chance to turn on their captors.

"This victory may yet turn to defeat," he said aloud.

French Rear, 12:17 p.m.

A man-at-arms stumbled past the count of Dammartin. An empty sword sheath flapped uselessly at his side. Other fugitives from the battle followed; all were close to collapse.

"Wait!" Dammartin leaned from his saddle, clutching at the man's shoulder.

The soldier looked up.

"What is happening?" the count demanded.

The man stared uncomprehendingly.

"Where are Marshal Boucicaut and Constable d'Albret?" Dammartin irritably shook the man.

"Dead," the soldier mumbled. "All dead."

"What?" Dammartin was stunned. "That cannot be so."

The man shook his head. "They're all dead. Every last one," he repeated.

Dammartin released his grip on the man's shoulder. "You heard? We must act," Dammartin hurled at Fauquembergue.

"We had better do it while we still have men," the other man replied.

Some of the horsemen were slipping away as uncertainty spread through the ranks of the mounted division. Others clamoured to fight, jeering at those riding off.

"We attack!" bellowed Fauquembergue, drawing his sword.

King Henry's Standard, 12:19 p.m.

Henry studied the massed French cavalry on the far side of the field. A single figure was riding up and down the lines of horsemen as if issuing orders. His own army had fragmented into small groups as men hunted for loot, food and water; others slumped wearily wherever there was empty ground amid the piles of bodies. He looked again at the thousands of French prisoners watched by just a handful of guards. The captives were the only large group of men on the English side of the battlefield.

"Kill the prisoners!" he calmly said.

Camoys and the other lords stared at the king; not a single man moved.

"Get the men back to their positions. Reform the battle line. And kill the prisoners," Henry raised his voice.

"Sire? Kill the prisoners?" Camoys asked. "But why?"

Henry pointed at the French cavalry.

"Those horsemen are readying to attack, and the enemy force that overran the camp may appear in our rear at any moment,"

Henry rapidly explained. "We will be caught between them. If the prisoners use the confusion to arm themselves, our men will be cut down before we can reform the army."

Several of the lords looked at the throng of prisoners, and the thousands of swords, lances and other abandoned weapons lying at their feet; the captives had only to pick them up and the English would be facing a new French army in their midst. All of the nobles grasped the king's reasoning, but none of them liked it.

"It is not honourable! They have yielded," Sir Gilbert Umfraville objected. "We cannot butcher defenceless men."

Henry coldly stared at the knight.

"Your pardon, sire," the giant mumbled. "I forget my place."

"Hear me," Henry snapped. "There is no time to debate morality, my lords. We are in mortal danger. You will kill the prisoners or they will kill us!"

None of the men around him moved.

"Many of the captives are nobles of high-born blood. If we kill them we will lose their ransoms," Camoys voiced what some of the others were thinking.

"And where will you count your money, my lord? In Heaven?" Henry retorted. "I will hear no more objections or arguments. Put the prisoners to the sword."

The nobles looked at each other, waiting for someone else to act. Henry grunted with impatience. Every second wasted arguing aided the enemy. He looked over the heads of the miserable men standing in front of him.

At that moment, Henry saw a company of archers forming up: it was the only organised body of men in the English army apart from his own guards. The king instantly recognised the tall captain hurrying the men into neat lines

"Selby," he said.

If anyone would keep his command together, the king thought, it was the dour northerner.

A knight brought Selby to the king's side moments later. The nobles moved aside, glad to escape Henry's attention.

"Master Selby, you have served me and the army well this day. I have heard how you helped lead the attacks on the French that turned the battle. And now you shall receive a harsh reward for your services," Henry greeted the archer bleakly.

"Sire," Selby said simply.

"The French still threaten us. Look." Henry pointed at the cavalry on the far side of the field. "If we are attacked the prisoners may turn on us, and we shall surely lose the day. Kill the captives."

"Aye, sire," Selby responded gruffly. He had grasped the king's reasoning at once.

"Every last man," Henry called after him as Selby turned back to his waiting company.

Selby made a point of killing the first prisoner himself. He strode up to the man, a knight, who watched him approach with a growing frown. The man's puzzlement turned to shock as Selby swung the club. There was a sharp crack as the knight's unprotected skull shattered. A second later Thomas Downer thrust a knife into the throat of the gaping man next to the knight. The archers behind waded into the stunned prisoners, cutting down the defenceless men with axes, swords and wooden hammers.

Selby's men had shown little taste for the task they had been given, but they were king's men, accustomed to obeying even the harshest orders. Wordlessly, the archers slashed and hacked at the prisoners. Some of the captives tried to ward off the blows with upraised arms or bare hands; they screamed as the falling blades and hammers severed flesh and splintered bones. Others tried to run, only to be blocked by the men cowering behind them.

"Stop! Stop! We yielded! Do not kill us!" some of the captives implored.

English soldiers from other companies gaped at the slaughter as their captains and sergeants hustled them past, driving them back to the battle line. Not a single man moved to join in the killing.

Henry unflinchingly watched the slaughter. Selby had two hundred men, and within minutes they had cut down at least a thousand prisoners. A few of the French snatched swords or other weapons from the ground and tried to fight, but most of the captives were too cowed or exhausted to act.

"This is not honourable, sire," Camoys protested.

"The French brought it on themselves," the king said. "You saw how they unfurled their sacred red banner. It was a declaration they would take no prisoners." Without turning, Henry gestured at the archers slaughtering the wailing prisoners. "Look well, my lord. But for fortune and God's mercy, that would have been you and I."

French Rear, 12:22 p.m.

The count of Fauquembergue railed at the line of sullen horsemen.

"Advance. I command you to advance?" he screamed.

A few of the riders edged their horses forwards, but most of the men did not move.

"What is wrong with you? Do you not see we must attack the enemy? Have you no honour?" Fauquembergue roared at those who hung back.

"What is the point of going to certain death?" one of the riders shot back. "See."

Fauquembergue looked where the man was pointing. Lines of archers were forming up where the English banners flapped in the chilly afternoon breeze.

"If we attack, the accursed English will kill us all with their hellish bows. We won't even get close," the rider said.

Others nodded or grunted agreement.

Fauquembergue's shoulders slumped. Despair and fatigue crashed down on him.

Dammartin looked enquiringly at him. "It is done?" he asked.

Fauquembergue nodded. "It is done."

Dammartin turned his horse's head and rode back through the horsemen. "Follow me," he commanded.

Wordlessly, the riders turned their backs on the English.

Fauquembergue stared across the field. The chivalry of France had perished in a single hour.

"And for what?" he asked the empty air.

King Henry's Standard, 12:23 p.m.

"Sire! The French horse. They are leaving." Umfraville excitedly pointed across the fields at the dispersing enemy cavalry.

The king looked at where the knight was pointing. Turning, he gestured at Selby's men slaughtering the French prisoners. "Stop them, Gilbert," Henry ordered.

Umfraville needed no further instruction. With remarkable speed for a man of his size, the knight dashed forwards.

"Stop! Selby, the king says stop," the knight called as he ran. "The danger has passed."

Selby looked up when he heard the shouts. He was standing over a kneeling man-at-arms, about to thrust a knife into the prisoner's bare neck. The captain saw Umfraville running towards him.

"Your lucky day, my friend." Selby released the prisoner.

"What?" the man asked uncomprehendingly in French.

The captain looked around. His sergeants were halting the killing, but hundreds of prisoners were dead. Selby glanced at the bewildered man crouching at his feet before answering in the simple French that he had learned in a lifetime of soldering.

"You live. We all live for another day."

English Lines, 1:10 p.m.

The English army had reassembled behind the rows of wooden stakes. Archers, with arrows plucked from the mud and the bodies of the French, once more lined the flanks with the men-at-arms in the centre.

At dawn the army had resembled starving, weather-beaten beggars. Now they looked more like the fiends who torment damned souls in church paintings of Hell. There was barely a man whose face, hands and clothing were not splattered with blood. Hungry and exhausted, the army waited wordlessly. Only the soldiers' ragged breathing broke the silence as the king rode along the ranks. He saw the weariness in their faces, their sagging shoulders, and arms hanging limply. But he also saw the swords, lances and bows clasped ready for use.

Henry rode back to the middle of the line and halted. Every man in the army looked at their monarch.

"We have won a great victory even though greatly outnumbered by a proud and cruel enemy who scorned us. I thank you for your service, and above all for your courage. We must not be too proud. If we prevailed it was because the Almighty in his great goodness gave us victory. How else could so few defeat so many?"

He paused for a moment to let the words sink in.

"This is a day that will be remembered for as long as England endures. As you will be remembered and honoured through all the long centuries to come. You shall never be forgotten."

Silence greeted the king's words, but every man would treasure them for the rest of his days.

"The danger is not done. We may yet be attacked. The army will hold its position," the king finished.

English Lines, 4:56 p.m.

The English army held its positions until the last of the afternoon light faded. Only then did Henry decide that the French would not come again. The contingents shuffled into the darkness.

As Henry watched the departing ranks, a group of horsemen loomed out of the dark. Several of the king's escorts drew their swords.

"The heralds, sire," Sir John Cornwall calmed the guards.

Henry greeted the English and French emissaries. They had watched the battle from the edge of the woods. The laws of chivalry and war required that the heralds rule on the events of the day even if no one could doubt what had just happened.

"Sire. The victory is yours," the French herald Montjoie spoke first. His voice was bleak.

"We thank you, good herald," the king answered. "Tell me, what is the name of this place?"

Henry knew the answer, but protocol had its requirements even in the middle of a bloodbath.

"The nearest manor is Agincourt, sire." Montjoie pointed to the stone tower on the far side of the battlefield.

"Then we shall call this fight in its name. It shall be known ever after as the Battle of Agincourt," Henry declared. "There are other matters, I fear, bloody matters," he added after a pause. "Sir John. You have the count of our losses?"

"Of all the miracles we have seen this day, this may be the greatest, sire," Cornwall replied. "Our losses are a handful despite the terrible slaughter. Only two of our great men, the duke of York and the young earl of Suffolk, are slain."

Cornwall looked at the men waiting on his next words.

"All told, we suffered about a hundred dead in the fighting," he concluded.

There were gasps of astonishment. Only the king received the news without surprise.

"Then you spoke truly, old friend. This is a miracle," he said. "But you do not speak of what happened in the camp."

Cornwall unhappily shook his head. "We are still taking a count, sire, but scores died, many of them boys."

Henry looked at Montjoie.

"And what of the French losses?" the king asked.

"At least ten thousand are dead. Much of the army is destroyed. Among the slain are some of the greatest princes and nobles in France. The whole country will weep."

The herald paused as if struggling to speak.

"I fear the true number of the dead will never be known," he added.

English Camp, 8:12 p.m.

Bands of soldiers and archers huddled beneath the bare trees or shivered under sodden blankets amid the wreckage of the English camp. Only a few had managed to kindle fires, and the damp sticks gave more smoke than heat. The army was numb with cold, exhaustion and hunger. There was no food, and only rainwater from muddy puddles to drink.

The deaths of some of the lords and knights might mean there was a little more space in the cottages and hovels occupied by the nobles, but the common men still had to shelter under the night sky.

Men glumly examined the fine swords, armour, jewels and purses full of coins and other treasures they had looted from French corpses.

"I'd give all of this for a bit of beef and a flagon of beer," grumbled one archer as he speculatively weighed a bulging leather sack of coins in his grubby hand.

"That's more money than you've seen in your life," his friend said.

"And I'd give it all for a crust of bread," the man retorted.

"You will lose it soon enough. First tavern we come to you'll squander it all on whores and wine."

Duke of Lancaster's Quarters, 8:34 p.m.

William Bradwardyn finished removing the entrails. The surgeon showed the two butchers from the royal kitchens where to cut. One of the men nervously sank his cleaver into an arm at the shoulder. The stroke was misjudged, and the blade caught.

"Careful. This is not a side of mutton. The duke of York must be treated with all due reverence, even if he is dead," the surgeon chided.

Both butchers nodded apprehensively. Neither had been happy when they were sent to work under the surgeon. They were even less pleased on learning their chore was to cut up the bodies of York and the earl of Suffolk. The corpses would be boiled down to the bones, which would be taken home for burial. It was a special privilege reserved only for the highest nobles; lesser men were buried where they fell.

"Let me help you." Bradwardyn deftly used a knife to separate the flesh of the arm from the shoulder until only the bone glimmered wetly in the candlelight.

"Now the cleaver. Only a single stroke is necessary," he instructed.

An hour later the smell of simmering flesh wafted to the soldiers outside the hut.

"Bastards! Why can't they spare a mouthful for us," one man muttered.

King Henry's Tent, 9:50 p.m.

A large wooden platter was placed in the centre of the table. Henry glanced at the shrivelled chicken, two small loaves of bread and a few stunted apples huddled in the centre of the plate, and then at the dozen men seated around the table. It was the last of the food in the royal larder.

The king's gaze turned to the man who had served the meagre meal.

"Our thanks," he said.

The duke of Orleans did not think he could feel any more shame, but the English king's words made his cheeks purple. The duke of Bourbon leaned forwards to pour wine into the king's cup.

Henry nodded to Orleans to serve the chicken to the English lords at the table. How could it come to this? Orleans thought, as he awkwardly carved the tough flesh. Two royal dukes of France waiting like kitchen lackeys on an English upstart.

"You are distressed, cousin?"

Orleans jerked up as the words broke his thoughts.

"You are distressed?" Henry repeated.

Orleans mumbled a denial.

"Come, cousin. You know the traditions of war. The defeated wait upon the victor at his table after the battle." Henry's tone was gentle.

"It is not honourable. We are of royal blood," Orleans blurted. Some of the English lords smirked at his misery.

"What you had planned for me was not honourable," Henry said coldly. "No one will parade you in a cart through the streets of London dressed only in a shirt."

Orleans and Bourbon looked startled. Henry gave a short laugh.

"Yes. We know of your plans for us had you won the battle."

Both men stared down at the floor, expecting a tirade or a blow.

"Cousins," Henry soothed. "There is no need for apprehension. You will be treated with respect for your rank and your blood."

The two men looked relieved. Orleans resumed his clumsy efforts to carve the fowl.

"What think you of the day?" Henry asked as the duke put a scrap of meat on the king's plate.

"It was a great victory for your majesty," Orleans stiffly replied.

"It was God's victory," Henry said.

PART V

THE DAYS AFTER

—— 26 OCTOBER ——

Agincourt, 9:32 a.m.

Thomas stared at the heap of French corpses; it was as high as his waist. Bodies lay piled on top of each other, the torsos, arms and legs intertwined; their eyes were open, staring at the living.

Similar mounds littered the battlefield. English archers, grooms and servants were pulling corpses from the heaps to be stripped and searched. Weapons were wrenched from lifeless hands, armour ripped from torsos and limbs, pockets and purses rifled for coins and jewels. After a cursory search, the now naked carcasses were tossed aside; no one thought of burying them.

"Here be one still breathing," a bowmen called. One of the bodies had moved when he had trodden on it. A captain overseeing the work turned to inspect the discovery.

The bowman put a hand on the knife hanging at his side and looked enquiringly at the captain.

The captain nodded.

The talk woke the wounded man. He saw the archer leaning over, and glimpsed the unsheathed blade. A faint, choking protest rose from his cracked lips.

"Stop! In the name of Heaven, stop!" Thomas rushed forwards, raising his hands.

The startled bowman pulled back the knife. The captain turned to see the monk.

"It is not right to kill a defenceless man. God forbids such things," Thomas protested.

"Brother, this is not your place." There was no anger or animosity in the captain's voice, just weariness.

"The man lives. We must tend to him," Thomas pleaded.

"And then what, brother?" the captain asked. "To lie here and rot in his own shit? We cannot take him. A wounded man may linger for two or three days if left on the field. It is kinder to finish him now."

"I know." Thomas suddenly sobbed. "But it does not seem right."

The captain looked at the monk. "Come. There is nothing you can do." He gently led Thomas away. The bowman watched their receding backs, and then looked down at the wounded Frenchman. The man was moaning; the archer could not tell if he was trying to say something.

"Hush, now," he soothed.

Gently, the archer pulled back the Frenchman's head and with a single clean stroke severed the jugular. For a moment he held the man by the shoulders, comforting him until he saw the life vanish from his eyes.

Henry and his lords rode slowly across the battlefield. Their horses carefully picked a path through the carpet of French bodies. None of the riders spoke; it seemed impossible that the little English army had done this.

After an hour the king led them back to the English camp. Along the way they rode past English soldiers loaded down with piles of weapons and armour they had taken from the dead. One man was trudging along with six swords suspended on his back;

a similar number of breastplates hung from his crooked arms, and he clutched a helmet in each hand.

"The men can't march like this," Henry said. "Issue orders. Each man will take only such weapons and armour as he needs for his own protection. Destroy everything else."

Lord Camoys nodded in acknowledgement. "A wise decision, sire, although one the men will not care for. They will see it as a loss to their purses."

"Better a hole in their purses than being left behind," interjected Sir Gilbert Umfraville.

Henry turned to the knight. "Sir Gilbert, how far to Calais?"

"It is forty-five miles, by the scouts' reckoning, sire."

"Can we cover it in two days?" the king asked.

"I fear not. Many of the horses were lost in the French raid on the camp. We will be slowed by our wounded, and most of the men have little energy after the battle and not eating for days. It will not be an easy journey." Umfraville paused. "And for all we know, another French army may be waiting for us," he added.

"Then we shall go and find out," Henry calmly responded.

Archers and men-at-arms wound their way down the narrow track leading north from Agincourt. Plumes of black smoke rose behind them from the barns where the captured French weapons and armour had been piled amid bales of straw and set ablaze. The filthy, haggard soldiers travelled slowly; many barely had the strength to walk. Scores were wounded; coarse strips of dirty linen and torn clothing roughly bound cuts and wounds. Some men hobbled along using spears and sticks as crutches. The most seriously injured lay in the handful of carts the army still possessed: there were moans and shrieks of pain as the solid wooden wheels shuddered along the rutted track, jarring the prostrate men.

Henry watched the army shuffle past. He was alone except for a single knight.

"They are different men after yesterday," Sir John Cornwall said.

"We are all different men, but are we better men?" Henry mused.

"Better and humbler, sire. No man can live through such carnage and not be humbled."

Henry looked at the old knight.

"I pray you are right," he said.

— 27 OCTOBER —

Ten Miles from Agincourt, 7:34 p.m.

Exhausted soldiers lay by the side of the road wherever their contingents had halted for the night. Few of the men made any attempt to raise tents or fashion shelters from branches; instead they shivered under their damp cloaks, trying to block out the cold and the gnawing in their empty bellies.

Henry walked through the army, flanked by two companions. He had been forced to call a halt even though they had covered just ten miles that day.

"We must make greater progress," Sir Gilbert Umfraville gloomily observed.

Sir John Cornwall sighed. "The men go as fast as they can. Many barely have the strength to stand, let alone march," he said.

Henry glanced over his shoulder at the two men. "They must march or perish in these fields," he said. "Tell the captains to rouse the army at dawn. Any man who is not ready or resists will be left behind."

—— 28 OCTOBER ——

Near St Omer, 2:46 p.m.

The scouts mutely shook their heads as they returned. Once again they had found only empty countryside and abandoned villages stripped of food or anything else that might aid the English.

"Even the birds have fled. It is like the end of the world," grunted their leader.

Sir John Cornwall seemed untroubled by the bleak report. "You saw no sign of French troops, and that's all that matters," he said. "The army is in no state to fight another battle."

Raising his right arm, the old knight motioned the vanguard to continue the march.

The weary, half-starved men moved forwards as word snaked down the column that once again there would be no food or shelter that night.

—— 29 OCTOBER ——

Ten-Mile Marker on the Road to Calais, 6:00 a.m.

"Hold! Name yourselves!"

A squadron of armoured horsemen blocked the bridge. Their visors were down, lances lowered for attack.

"Who asks?" came the reply from the other side of the river.

"Are you from the king's army?" A man advanced from the front rank of the horsemen.

"King Henry's army, if that is your meaning," was the reply.

The mounted man clattered over the narrow stone bridge, pulling up before the band of archers.

"Truly, you are King Henry's men?" he anxiously asked.

"That we are," replied Robert Alderton, lowering his bow. He gestured to his men to do likewise.

"We had news that the French were searching for you, and feared the worse."

"They found us," Alderton said.

"What happened? Is the king alive?" the rider demanded.

A moment of silence was broken by laughter from the archers. The mounted man stared as if he had met a band of lunatics. Alderton held up his hand in a conciliatory gesture.

"The king is alive and victorious," he said.

"Victorious? You mean there was a battle?"

"A great battle. And the king did triumph."

The cavalry commander gaped. "You defeated the French army? But we did hear that the French sent a vast host against the king."

Alderton's smile slipped. "All of France challenged us. They came in the thousands and we slew them by the thousands. No man knows how many died. I only know that it was a victory the likes of which none has ever seen."

The rider greeted the news with stunned disbelief.

"Is this Calais?" Alderton asked.

"No, you are still ten miles from the city. The river marks the boundary of English territory. We have watched here for three days for any sign of the king."

The cavalry commander stared at Alderton and his scarecrow ruffians.

"How did you defeat the French?" he wonderingly asked.

"With this." Alderton raised his longbow. With his free hand he gestured at the wretches behind him. "And with these."

Calais, 2:00 p.m.

Henry of England entered the port of Calais in the early afternoon. Every soul of the garrison and the town cheered the king as he rode through the main gate with his lords. Scores of captured French nobles walked dejectedly behind them.

Word of the victory at Agincourt had whipped through the town. Calais had feared the king had been defeated, and the French would celebrate by attacking the port.

Henry rode to the castle, where the earl of Warwick, the city commander, and his lieutenants greeted him in the courtyard of the great fortress.

"Sire, it is a miracle that you are safe," exclaimed the earl.

Servants bustled about with refreshments as the officers of the garrison fired questions about the battle at the king's companions.

Henry slowly sipped a cup of wine and asked for news of England.

"Will you see your rooms now, sire?" Warwick asked after a time.

"Thank you. First we must see to quarters for our guests." The king motioned to the French prisoners morosely watching the cheerful English.

"Of course, sire. We heard that the dukes of Orleans and Bourbon are among the prisoners."

"And many more. The ladies of France will have to learn to dance with each other," Camoys laughingly interjected.

Outside the Walls of Calais, 9:12 p.m.

"It's not right," John Hampton complained. "We archers won the battle. But our high and mighty betters don't bother their heads about us now the killing is done."

Robert Alderton sighed. "It is the way of the world, John."

All around them the men of their company were improvising shelters from cloaks and ragged blankets on a stretch of waste ground outside the city walls. A piercing wind from the nearby sea beat against the feeble coverings.

Only the king, his nobles and knights had been admitted to the city, together with their French captives. Calais might have cheered news of the victory at Agincourt, but its residents did not like the idea of thousands of rough common soldiers sharing their town, and the army had been refused entry.

"Is this what we fought for?" Hampton demanded, refusing to be quietened. "To be treated like thieves and beggars?"

"We fought because we chose to; no one forced us," Alderton retorted. "And we showed that we are the equal of any man."

EPILOGUE

Calais Docks, 9:58 a.m.

Sailors swarmed over the wooden ship, preparing to put out to sea. Barrels were rolled up a thick plank from the quayside as bales were lowered into the hold. Soldiers in iron helmets peered from the fighting towers at either end of the ship.

A small group of passengers stood on the quayside waiting to board. Several knights talked loudly of the pleasures of going home to England; two merchants discussed London market prices; and a noble woman in grey travelling clothes stood silently with her maids. No one paid any attention to the tall young monk watching the green waves slap against the stone quay.

"Thomas!" A booming voice silenced the chatter. A short, muscular figure strode past the momentarily distracted passengers and embraced the monk.

"What's this, lad?" Sir John Cornwall demanded. "This is no time to be leaving."

Thomas smiled. "Sir John. I had not thought to see you again. You are much taken up with the king's business these days."

"I dropped everything to dash down here when the king's chaplain told me that you were leaving."

"I left a note at your quarters," the monk began to explain.

"Then we can read it together when we go back there," Sir John cut him off.

Thomas blushed, awkwardly hanging his head. "You don't understand," he stammered.

"Nonsense. You can't leave. I need you here. Stay and be my chief clerk. What do you say to that?"

"It would be an honour, Sir John," the monk said.

"More work than honour. I've a dozen French lords to be ransomed. Do you have any idea of how much haggling that will take? It will mean a mountain of letter-writing. Ideal employment for a good priest," the knight happily continued. "What do you say?"

Thomas slowly shook his head.

"But why, Thomas? It is an honourable task, and you will be well recompensed," the puzzled knight asked.

"Thank you, Sir John. But I must return to the monastery."

Sir John studied Thomas. "What is it, lad? Are you ill?"

"No, I am well. Or at least no physical ailment troubles me."

"What then? Tell me."

"I have seen terrible things. So many dead. So much suffering. I no longer know what to think," the monk said.

"Ah." The knight's smile faded. "I see."

"I need to pray and think. I need the wisdom and comfort of my brothers. I must try to comprehend everything that has happened."

"I forget sometimes that you are not used to war."

"How can anyone be used to it?"

"War is a part of life, Thomas," Cornwall spoke sombrely. "Many love it, and some cannot live without it."

"I could never become used to it," Thomas blurted.

"War deals out many kinds of injury. It wounds the mind as well as the body. And I see now that you are sorely afflicted. I hope the peace of your cloisters will heal you."

Thomas could only nod in reply. At that moment the ship's captain leaned over the guardrail and bellowed at the passengers to board. The waiting knights stood back to allow the noblewoman to go first while the merchants hurriedly checked their bags.

"Our time together has meant much to me, Thomas," Cornwall said.

"And I, Sir John." The monk brightened. "I shall never forget it."

"Worry not, brother. These clouds that oppress your spirits will lift in time."

"We have seen great things, Sir John."

"We have seen deeds that men will speak of for as long as England stands."

"How could so few defeat so many?"

Cornwall shook his head. "Ah, Thomas. Men will debate that for a hundred years and more."

"Was it the king?" the monk pressed.

"Henry is a great king, but it was the men. That rabble of archers with a handful of men-at-arms is one of the greatest armies the world has ever seen. They are the sweepings of peasants' hovels and the back alleys of the towns led by captains almost as poor and ill bred as they are. All of them expected to die that morning, and yet they stood their ground because they were fighting for everything that they love: the king, their kin, their honour and each other. That made us invincible."

All of the other passengers had boarded the ship. Two sailors waited to draw up the gangplank.

"You'd better go, lad," Cornwall broke the hush. He embraced the monk, and stepped back. Thomas smiled, turned and walked to the ship. Both men knew they would never see each other again.